Alternatives to the Peace Corps

A Directory of Third World & U.S. Volunteer Opportunities

Edited by
Phil Lowenthal,
Stephanie Tarnoff
and Lisa David

Oakland, CA: Food First Books

FOOD FIRST

The Institute for Food and Development Policy, popularly known as Food First, is a nonprofit research, analysis, and education-for-action center that exposes the social costs of orthodox development strategies and proposes alternative visions for participatory, equitable, and sustainable development.

To order additional copies of this book or receive a free catalog of resources call or write:

Food First Books
Subterranean Company
Box 160, 265 South 5th Street
Monroe, OR 97465

Tel: (503) 847-5274   Fax: (503) 847-6018
To Order Call Toll Free: 800-274-7826

Add $4.00 for postage and handling
Bulk discounts available

Copyright 1986, 1987, 1988, 1990, 1992, 1994, 1996
Institute for Food and Development Policy
Seventh edition, 1996
ISBN 0-935028-69-2

Library of Congress Catalog-in-Publication Data

Alternatives to the Peace Corps: a directory of Third World & U.S.
    volunteer opportunities / edited by Phil Lowenthal, Stephanie
    Tarnoff and Lisa David — 7th ed.
    ISBN 0-935028-69-2: $9.95
    1. Voluntarism — Directories.   2. Community Development
    — Directories
    I. Phil Lowenthal, Stephanie Tarnoff and Lisa David
    HN49. V64A47   1996
    361.3'7' 025 — dc20   96-19234
                                                            CIP

Cover Photo by: Doctors Without Borders. Taken during a medical relief trip in Vardenis, Armenia.

Printed by: Patterson Printers

TABLE OF CONTENTS

ACKNOWLEDGEMENTS

*A*lternatives to the Peace Corps is published in response to the numerous inquiries Food First receives from individuals seeking opportunities to gain community development experience.

Becky Buell, a staff member at Food First from 1985 to 1988, researched and wrote the original edition in 1986 with the assistance of Kari Hamerschlag, a Food First intern. Tremendous demand for the booklet created a continuing need to revise and update it periodically.

This seventh edition was revised and updated by Food First interns Phil Lowenthal, Stephanie Tarnoff and Lisa David, under the supervision of staff member Kathleen McClung. Deborah Toler made a significant contribution to the revised introduction. Design and production services were provided by Lory Poulson and Harvest Graphics. The cover photograph was contributed by Doctors Without Borders.

This book is made possible by the volunteers and friends who provide updates and additions each year. Many thanks go to the returned Peace Corps volunteers who have offered their perspectives in the development of this guide.

FOREWORD

Since 1961, more than 140,000 Americans have worked abroad through the Peace Corps voluntary service program. Thousands more have been volunteers with church, government, and private organizations.

What draws so many to dedicate years of their lives to voluntary service? Media images of famine are only the most vivid reminders of the wide discrepancies between our own standard of living and that of the world's majority. Many people, outraged by the injustice of world hunger and poverty, choose to apply themselves directly to solutions.

But how can we be assured that our actions are truly helping impoverished people? What is an appropriate role for outsiders working to end hunger and poverty abroad?

Every voluntary service organization has its own answers to these questions. While most use similar phrases — helping the poor to help themselves, building local self reliance, or inspiring participatory development — each organization has its own understanding of the causes of poverty and the volunteer's role in addressing those problems.

At the Institute for Food and Development Policy (Food First), we have found that world hunger is complicated by misunderstanding and false assumptions about effective solutions. Our analyses of food and population patterns throughout the world have led us to conclude that hunger is not a problem of scarcity, overpopulation, or natural disasters. Neither is hunger caused by poor people's lack of know-how. Rather, hunger is rooted in a system of food production, distribution, and consumption that concentrates control and benefits in the hands of a few.[1]

Once we recognize that hunger is not created by deficiencies on the part of the poor, our role as outsiders changes. Rather than seeing ourselves as problem solvers bringing our knowledge, we see ourselves as participants in a process of change that can be defined locally. We can contribute to this process in many ways if we understand that solutions must originate from the people who will be most affected.

Alternatives to the Peace Corps brings together resources and information that will help the prospective volunteer find an appropriate placement; one that is supportive of indigenous, community-based development. This guide is Food First's response to frequent requests for guidance on how to work with others to build more equitable societies. Many of these requests have come from people, some of them returned Peace Corps volunteers, who believe that U.S. foreign policy has been more damaging than helpful in the Third World. They question the links between U.S. foreign and military policy and the Peace Corps. *Alternatives to the Peace Corps* is the first guide of its kind to address directly these questions and offer alternative options for voluntary service.

WHY VOLUNTEER?

Before making a commitment, it is important to clarify your motives. You may be drawn to voluntary service by a desire to help impoverished people. You may be interested in learning about another culture and society. You may wish to be part of a process of positive social change. Or you may be eager to gain experience that will help you find employment. Each of these motivations will direct you to distinct options for voluntary service.

Humanitarian motivations lead many prospective volunteers to regions plagued by extreme poverty and injustice. While a volunteer may wish to feed the hungry, heal the sick or house the homeless, these social and political problems are often more complex than they might seem. Learning the dynamics of a community is the greatest challenge to a volunteer. Thus, the volunteer's most appropriate role is that of a student. Working abroad can better your understanding of the world and the forces that keep people impoverished, and enhance your appreciation of the richness of other cultures. These lessons can have a long-lasting impact on your life. For many, volunteer experience marks the beginning of a lifelong commitment to ending poverty and hunger. This resource guide to volunteer opportunities provides a listing of groups that work to support development as defined by local people.

Another motivation for voluntary service is the desire to learn more about societies. Living in another culture is an excellent way to build your understanding of the world and the structures that perpetuate poverty. Volunteering is one way to gain a firsthand perspective on community development. There are also educational programs specifically designed for students regarding culture and development. For example, work brigades, study tours, and international education programs offer short-term exposure. In this resource guide, several reputable tour programs are listed.

If your concern is to improve your qualifications for a career in development, an unconventional work experience may enhance your candidacy. The best programs place volunteers with indigenous non-governmental organizations (NGO) that have requested a volunteer for a specific purpose. In these circumstances, volunteers have a better chance of making a meaningful contribution. These placements, however, often require some skills—computer, teaching, agriculture, appropriate technology, health care, or fundraising. It would be wise to develop a specific technical skill, as well as language skills, which you know may be of use to an organization in another country.

If you feel particularly concerned and motivated to support the development of communities, a first step is to look at the connections between poverty and policy. The causes of poverty are multiple and complex, and are often related to policies of our government which have a profound impact on the poor. For example, U.S. military assistance to the Salvadoran government over the past decade perpetuated economic disparities and human rights abuses that have hindered development for poor communities. Economic policies handed down from the World Bank and the International Monetary Fund (IMF) in attempts to "modernize," have pushed poor farmers away from growing basic food crops, forcing them into export production that is both economically risky and environmentally unsound.

By pressuring for U.S. policies that are more accountable to the poor, we can help create a political climate in which grassroots efforts can flourish both here and abroad. Work in developing nations can deepen our understanding of this responsibility and, therefore, make our work at home more effective.

At Food First, we remind concerned U.S. citizens who want to help impoverished people that they may not need to travel around the globe to fulfill their goals. Often the best place to start is here at home where the challenges of community development are immense. One section of this resource guide is dedicated to U.S. organizations. Voluntary service in low-income communities in the U.S. can also be a valuable educational experience or preparation for future work.

LESSONS FROM THE PEACE CORPS

Deciding to volunteer is a difficult decision. Knowing why you want to is the first step toward choosing among the myriad options of where to go, with what organization, and with what funds.

The most common solution to this dilemma is to choose a volunteer program such as the "Peace Corps of the United States" where all arrangements are made by the sponsoring organization. Many such organizations provide training, health and accident insurance, travel expenses, and even a stipend.

This solution seems simple enough. But these programs are not always as straightforward as they seem. The choice of countries in which an organization works, the projects it supports, and the role of its volunteers have many political, social, and cultural implications. Volunteers are more than well-meaning individuals. They are representatives of the organizations that sponsor them. As such, volunteers are expected to communicate the governmental, religious, or institutional values and objectives of the organization they represent.

For example, the Peace Corps, the most renowned of the voluntary service organizations, is an agency of the U.S. government. The Peace Corps volunteer is part of the national team dispatched by the U.S. State Department, and accountable to the U.S. ambassador in the foreign country. As such, the Peace Corps is inevitably linked to U.S. foreign policy objectives, as is the Peace Corps volunteer.

The Peace Corps was established in 1961 by President John F. Kennedy as a means to build America's benevolent image at home and overseas. This image, however, was from the outset tainted by the underlying foreign policy manipulations of the program. One explicit goal of the Peace Corps was to counter Soviet cultural and political influence in the Third World. The role of volunteers in this effort is reflected in amendment 8(c) of the Peace

Corps legislation which orders that trainees be instructed in the "philosophy, strategy, tactics, and menace of Communism."

The Peace Corps was positioned within the U.S. State Department where "the foreign policy of the United States is best served."[2] Despite the humanitarian goals expressed by the Peace Corps' first director, Sargent Shriver, there was a clear link between U.S. foreign and military policy and the placement of Peace Corps volunteers. The internal contradictions of the Peace Corps became most evident during the war in Vietnam when volunteers began speaking out against U.S. military intervention in the Third World. Volunteers in Guatemala, Panama, the Dominican Republic and South Korea sent a petition expressing their objections. "The President's verbal endorsement of the accomplishments and ideals of the Peace Corps is a hypocritical use of this organization," wrote the volunteers. "The government is using us as apologists for policies that run counter to the reasons for our service."[3] Other protests in Chile, Ecuador, Tunisia and Ethiopia led to efforts by Congress and the Administration to quiet the volunteers when their beliefs ran contrary to administration policy.[4]

The ideological underpinnings of the Peace Corps have evolved to reflect the changing nature and objectives of U.S. foreign policy. In the 1980s the largest number of Peace Corps volunteers were placed in countries like Grenada, Honduras and the Philippines where the U.S. military had a strong presence. The Peace Corps' work in these settings was effective in offsetting the negative image and impact of this strong U.S. military presence. According to one former Peace Corps country director, "In deciding the allocations of volunteers, we were aware of a formula which calculated the ratio of military personnel to civilians in a country. If the military presence skewed the ratio, the number of Peace Corps volunteers would be increased to create a more balanced presence."

With the end of the Cold War, the Peace Corps has evolved to fit the new character of U.S. foreign policy. In the 1990s the U.S.

government clearly defined the battle lines in the Third World in economic terms. By influencing the patterns of resource control, legislation, and monetary policy within Third World countries, whether through International Monetary Fund (IMF) imposed structural adjustment programs or free trade agreements, the U.S. government has found new ways to keep the Third World "safe for capitalism." In the 1990s U.S. policy is no longer defined primarily by military influence, but rather by its ability to mold societies through economic intervention.

The Peace Corps fits neatly into this new form of intervention in the Third World. Under the leadership of former director Loret Miller Ruppe, the Peace Corps began billing itself less as a symbol of good will and more seriously as a development agency. Through initiatives such as the African Food System Initiative and the Small Enterprise Development Program, Peace Corps volunteers began promoting private enterprise and the development of export production in the rural sector. The development of these programs coincided with the International Monetary Fund's structural adjustment programs which forced Third World governments to cut price supports for production of basic grains. The net impact of these changes eroded the standing of poor farmers. Countries like Honduras now import basic grains such as corn and beans and small farmers find themselves carrying debt as they move into export production.

In 1992 the Peace Corps began establishing a presence in the Republics of the former Soviet Union and Eastern Europe. The goal of this program is to support small business development and privatization of the state controlled economies. Volunteers placed include economists, accountants, bankers and specialists in advertising, marketing, business planning, management and privatization. Observers note that the Peace Corps is now "fulfilling a 26-year-old goal of having Americans help transform the communist states into capitalist democracies."[5] Former Peace Corps director, Elaine Chao, sees this move as putting the Peace Corps on "freedom's new frontier."[6]

From the Volunteer's Perspective

Many Peace Corps volunteers would argue that their placement had little or nothing to do with the larger policy objectives of the U.S. government. One volunteer working in the mountain region of the Philippines had no contact with the Peace Corps office, U.S.AID, or any other Peace Corps volunteer in his two years of service. "I arrived at the community and worked out my role with them," he explained.

Most volunteers feel that their service had a positive impact independent of the other agencies and policy initiatives of the U.S. government. "I worked with women to develop composting techniques and planting vegetables," said a volunteer working in Honduras. "These are techniques that will benefit them for a lifetime."

While some Peace Corps volunteers have struggled for years to keep their work autonomous from U.S. government policy (volunteers protested director Paul Coverdell's move to rename the organization The United States Peace Corps), the link is inherent. Congress has repeatedly expressed the link. "If there is a person in the Peace Corps who feels he cannot support U.S. foreign policy, then he ought not to be in the Peace Corps," stated Sen. Ross Adair (R-Ind).[7]

Keeping one's views silent may be more difficult in some countries than in others. A volunteer in Honduras, for example, was told it was unacceptable to express opinions contrary to U.S. policy in that country. In Tanzania, however, Peace Corps volunteers felt the program was not complicated by larger geo-political interests. Prospective volunteers should look closely at their placement and determine how their views may be inhibited by their affiliation.

Despite all the concerns about the Peace Corps as an arm of U.S. foreign policy, the agency must be credited with enabling thousands of American citizens to see firsthand the realities of poverty and injustice in the Third World. Most Peace Corps volunteers will attest that living and working alongside poor communities was the most powerful experience of their lives, one that has influenced their decisions and actions since. Many returned Peace Corps volunteers have learned through their placement the intimate connections between development and economic justice, militarization and human rights. They return to the U.S. and work to make U.S. foreign and domestic policy more accountable to the poor.

As one returned Peace Corps volunteer explained, "If there is one thing to thank the Peace Corps for, it's for showing me how U.S. policies hurt the average person. In a country like Paraguay, it is hard to miss the connection between U.S. aid and the oppression of the poor; it's hard to miss the links between the IMF economic package and the inability of the poor to feed themselves. These realizations radically changed my perspectives on the world."[8]

[1] See Food First's books, *World Hunger: Twelve Myths,* by Frances Moore Lappé and Joseph Collins; *Taking Population Seriously,* by Frances Moore Lappé and Rachel Schurman, and *Kerala: Radical Reform as Development in an Indian State,* by Richard W. Franke and Barbara H. Chasin.

[2] The Peace Corps Act, Public Law 87-293, Title 1, "Declaration of Purpose," September, 1961.

[3] Bent K. Ashabranner, *A Moment in History: The First Ten Years of the Peace Corps* (Garden City, NY: Doubleday, 1971), pp. 295-99.

[4] For firsthand accounts by Peace Corps volunteers of the conflicts associated with volunteering with a U.S. government agency, see Karen Schwarz, *What You Can Do for Your Country: An Oral History of the Peace Corps* (New York: William Morrow Company, 1991).

[5] Bill McAllister, "Peace Corps Plans to Send 500 to Ex-Soviet States," *The Washington Post,* December 31, 1991, p. A11.

[6] Elaine L. Chao, "Today's Peace Corps," address to National Press Club, Washington, D.C., May 5, 1992.

[7] As quoted in Schwarz, ibid, p. 103.

[8] Personal interview with returned Peace Corps volunteer who asked to remain anonymous.

OPTIONS FOR VOLUNTEERING

Once you have clarified your personal objectives, it's time to consider what type of placement makes the most sense for you. Listed in the resource guide are a number of established agencies and programs that offer service opportunities in a wide range of countries and settings. You may also consider one of the following alternatives that may be more appropriate for your particular interests.

Designing Your Own Experience

Some of the most exciting possibilities for working abroad can be designed independently according to your interests and beliefs. One option is to identify a group or organization and communicate directly about working as a volunteer. By researching grassroots organizations, you will learn more about the needs of organizations and the skills you may have to offer.

Identifying local grassroots organizations calls for thorough investigative research. You can begin by reviewing alternative publications, development journals, and the annual reports of organizations that fund projects such as Oxfam, Grassroots International, International Development Exchange (IDEX), or the Global Fund for Women. We have listed several publications in the resource guide that catalog grassroots organizations throughout the world. This is only the first step.

You will need to contact organizations to determine whether they would be interested in hosting a volunteer. Clearly state your goals and expectations, skills you offer and length of time you are available. The organization can then decide if you can be of service in their work.

Learning as a Student

Another option is to go overseas as a student. A number of universities offer study abroad programs that provide an opportunity to learn about the political, economic and social climates of a given country. Once you are established in a country, you can seek out individuals and groups directly involved with community development. They may be able to direct you to an appropriate volunteer placement where you can build your skills and experience in community development.

Short-term Opportunities

A long-term commitment may not be necessary. If your goal is to gain a better understanding of the world and to learn from the experiences of others, another option is to choose one or several short-term trips or work exchange programs. There are a number of groups that conduct exposure tours in the Third World. These are socially responsible, educational tours that provide participants firsthand experience of the political, economic and social structures that create or promote hunger, poverty and environmental degradation. Tours offer an opportunity to meet people with diverse perspectives on agriculture, development and the environment. They often include the opportunity to stay with local people, visit rural areas, and meet with grassroots organizers. Such tours can alter your understanding of hunger and poverty and direct you to areas where you can best work for democratic social change.

In any case, whether you choose an organized volunteer program, a tour, or go on your own, it is essential to do your homework beforehand. Read as much as possible about the country including its political climate, learn about groups working in the area, write in advance to groups that interest you, and talk to people at home who know about the area you are considering.

COMMON QUESTIONS

How can I finance my stay if I don't go through an established program?

For many people, financing is the greatest obstacle. It is often the primary reason for going through a government or church organization. Many Peace Corps volunteers are attracted by the option to defer student loans during the period of their placement. In fact, student loans can be deferred while participating in any volunteer agency.

While some agencies offer a stipend, insurance and travel, many smaller programs are not able to offer these benefits. However, there are alternative funding sources to consider for overseas work. Scholarships, fellowships or loans are also available. You may find funds to pay travel expenses by going through a university or language-study program. Some university departments have research funds that are available to both undergraduate and graduate students. A public library, a career service center, or a specialized library like the Foundation Center—with branches throughout the country—are sources for information on grants and loans.

There are many other untapped resources in local governments, private associations and church groups. The Rotary Club, for example, offers scholarships for foreign travel. Many churches will support their parishioners in return for educational service upon return from an overseas trip.

Friends and relatives are another possible source of funds. You may be able to arrange a personal loan or an exchange. One woman who traveled throughout Central America for a year started her own newsletter and asked friends and family to subscribe to help subsidize her living expenses.

The first source may be your own bank account. Look at the possibility of working to save money for a trip. The primary expense will be your airfare. Living in the Third World, especially in rural areas, can be extremely affordable. If you can arrange an internship or a work exchange (e.g., teaching English) for room and board, your living expenses can be kept to a minimum.

Do I need technical skills?

Generally, the demand for unskilled volunteers is low. While groups like the Peace Corps offer opportunities for "generalists," organizations with a longer term commitment to development in a given area may require specialized skills not available locally. In considering volunteer opportunities, it's important to ask if you would be taking a job that could be done by a local person. If you are offering a new skill to an area, you should investigate whether the program involves transferring that skill to local people.

In any work experience local people can best define your role. Let them know what your skills are and allow them to decide how they can best put those skills to use. Someone who went to work with a community organization in Mexico learned that his most useful skill was puppet-making. He didn't know before he arrived that street theater is a popular form of political communication. When a local clinic learned that he was an artist and an actor, they suggested he help them communicate health care information through puppet shows. There are many organizations that take volunteers for specific technical skills, such as construction, health care and agriculture.

Do I have to be Christian to be a volunteer with one of the church agencies?

Most major national and international religious organizations have a development agency or aid program; some have volunteer programs. It is important to establish whether an agency sees its primary purpose as social or evangelical. Some may ask that volunteers participate in a structured religious community, others may ask that volunteers participate in some evangelical work.

Consult an organization's brochures and materials to determine their expectations.

Listed in the resource guide are some volunteer programs with religious affiliations. We have selected programs that hold as their primary purpose the support of local efforts at community development. Some do require a commitment to a certain faith, but most ask only that the volunteer share a concern for social justice. As with any volunteer placement, it is important to understand the values behind an agency's volunteer program clearly.

What are the possibilities for getting paid work overseas?

Most overseas development positions require two or more years of community development experience. However, a two-year volunteer post does not guarantee future employment and is not the only way to gain sufficient experience. A woman who worked as a freelance journalist in Central America now works with the World Wildlife program in the region. A director of alternative tours became a grants manager at a U.S.-based agency. You may find that by developing your skills and connections with Third World communities, your job possibilities open up. In the reference section, you will find organizations and publications that list employment openings overseas.

Will my work displace a local person from a paid job?

You should be aware that you may well encounter hostility from local people who could easily be employed doing the work you are doing. Recent IMF and World Bank structural adjustment policies have demanded the "downsizing" of Third World governments. As a result, thousands of highly educated and skilled civil servants have lost their jobs. "Privatization" and trade "liberalization" have also thrown a number of skilled people in the private sector out of work.

Seeing no other viable alternative, many of these now unemployed professionals have returned to rural communities to farm. This means in both urban and rural settings you may run into people who will want to know why you are taking a job away from local people.

On the one hand, after thinking about this tough ethical issue — for whether you are a volunteer or paid, you will more than likely be filling a job a national could be doing — you may decide to stay in the U.S. and work on poverty and hunger issues here. But, on the other hand, you can also decide to go overseas prepared to endure and respond to a justified hostility.

The fact is that we do need progressive Americans who have gained some first hand knowledge of the cultural richness and complexity of Third World cultures. In the first place, Third World societies are too often portrayed in our media and our universities' "development" courses as hopeless basketcases. These portrayals provide legitimation for intrusive and detrimental U.S. policies.

Americans are probably in the best position to understand the nuances of American cultural arrogance and American racism that shape these images. So it is important to have a cadre of progressive Americans who can take their Third World experiences and, in light of their understanding of American societal attitudes, craft the most effective criticisms of U.S. policies.

Second, precisely because of that American racism and cultural narcissism, the unfortunate truth is that American audiences are more likely to be swayed by a "fellow American" than by a Third World national decrying the negative impact of U.S. policies. But, at the same time, American audiences demand that "been there" stamp of credibility in order to hear your message.

And third, it is clear that contemporary economic globalization requires a globalization of citizens' responses to its economic devastation. Cross cultural experiences via Third World people with living experiences in the West and vice versa are important to building this global citizens' movement.

In short, if you decide to work in a Third World country, know that you may well be displacing a Third World national from a much needed job. Be prepared for the possibility of being yelled at for your presence. Be confident in your own mind that the benefits to your overall political and ethical objectives are worth the price of that justified anger.

And if you encounter such hostility, be willing to admit its validity and be prepared to try to make your case about why getting this experience was so important. Changing U.S. government policies regarding foreign aid allocations, trade barriers to Third World exports, and transnational corporations is, in the end, the only way to ensure all of us access to environmentally sustainable living-wage jobs.

EVALUATING AN ORGANIZATION

No matter which voluntary service organization you are considering, get answers to questions such as these before you make a commitment:

- What is the political or religious affiliation of the organization? Is the purpose of the organization to convert or influence poor people to adopt new cultural, economic or social values?

- Who funds the organization? Do the funding sources have political or religious affiliations that may influence the organization's programs?

- Is the organization working with local or national governments? Overtly or covertly? Under the auspices of another institution?

- In what countries does the organization have programs? In what countries does it NOT have programs, and why?

These questions are hard to answer with the information supplied in brochures or publicity materials. Look beyond the brochures. Get a list of program alumni and ask them about their experiences, write to people in the field, find out who is critical of the program and why. The reference section lists several books that take a critical look at development organizations overseas.

BRINGING THE LESSONS HOME

L iving abroad and working with poor communities to confront the causes of hunger and poverty can have a long-lasting impact on your life. It can also deepen your understanding of the tremendous power the U.S. has over the lives of people around the world: power to make and break governments; to affect the world economy through trade, investment, and foreign aid policies; and to influence economic priorities through international aid programs such as U.S. AID, the World Bank and the International Monetary Fund.

Going abroad will be educational, but that is only the beginning. Experience with a disenfranchised community means taking the responsibility of bringing your experiences home. The lessons learned abroad may have direct applications: working to end hunger and poverty in our own country, pressuring the U.S. government to end its involvement with repressive regimes, stopping the militarization of the Third World, and holding U.S. corporations accountable for their actions abroad.

There are many ways in which a Third World experience can be translated into work at home. A Peace Corps volunteer who served with Guatemalan Indians returned to the U.S. and worked with Native Americans in Arizona. A health care volunteer with an international organization in Ghana found work at a free clinic in California. An agricultural extension worker who volunteered in Mozambique became active in the movement to stop U.S. support of South Africa's apartheid regime. These examples and others show that experience in a marginalized community is often the catalyst for taking action in our own country to create more democratic organizations and policies at the local, national, and international levels, and to help ensure the survival of grassroots efforts all over the world.

HOW THIS LIST WAS SELECTED

In compiling the following list of organizations we looked for groups that are addressing the political and economic causes of poverty. In our view, these programs place volunteers in positions that complement the work of local people, grassroots organizations, and non-governmental organizations (NGO). Many on the list are not traditional voluntary service organizations. They may have programs that send volunteers abroad, but their main purpose is educational work in the U.S. Through service and work projects, their aim is to build lasting links between communities at home and abroad.

The listings are by no means comprehensive. Many organizations are so small and take so few volunteers that they preferred not to be listed. Hundreds of other possibilities are not mentioned because they are not formal volunteer programs. Every community, school, church, and labor union has the potential for developing international programs that send delegates abroad, initiate ongoing partnership programs, and offer direct assistance to Third World communities. These opportunities are often the most exciting, but must be created by the volunteer.

The resource guide provides a starting point to explore the options for volunteering. Through your own research of these organizations and others, you can choose the appropriate options available to you.

Alternatives to the Peace Corps is an ongoing project of Food First. This guide will be updated again in the future. We rely on the comments and recommendations of our readers to improve each new edition. We welcome your suggestions for changes or additions.

> **Note: Most of the organizations listed in the resource guide function on very small budgets. If you are writing to request information, please enclose a self-addressed, stamped envelope.**

INTERNATIONAL VOLUNTARY
SERVICE ORGANIZATIONS

The following organizations offer opportunities to work with impoverished people in the Third World. These voluntary service organizations were selected for a common approach to combating poverty, one which emphasizes support of grassroots efforts to empower poor people.

American Friends Service Committee

1501 Cherry Street
Philadelphia, PA 19102-1479
Tel: (215) 241-7295   Fax: (215) 241-7247
Telex: 247 559 AFSC UR
Cable: AFSERCO Philadelphia

American Friends Service Committee (AFSC) sponsors summer programs in Cuba and Mexico for people ages 18 to 26. The Cuba program consists of a 3-week summer work project on small farms near Havana. Participants help with crop care and maintenance and attend a youth conference during the last week of the program. The cost is variable.

The Mexico program runs from late-June to mid-August. Participants live and work in rural villages and respond to the needs of the particular community in which they live. Applicants should have skills in construction, gardening, arts, crafts, child care, or other practical areas. Participants pay a $900 fee and cover the cost of their own travel expenses. Proficiency in Spanish is necessary for both programs. A limited number of scholarships are available.

Amigos de las Americas

5618 Star Lane
Houston, TX 77057
Tel: (800) 231-7796
http:\\www.amigoslink.org

In this program, volunteers 16 years or older work in teams in Latin America. They provide health services at schools, health clinics, and in communities. In addition to bringing technical knowledge and supplies to the project, the volunteers assume leadership roles as health educators. A network of Amigos chapters and training groups across the U.S. conducts training prior to departure and raises funds for the majority of volunteers. Costs range from $2,685 to $3,200, depending on the area of placement. This covers all expenses including housing with a family. At least 1 year of Spanish is a prerequisite. There are currently programs in Mexico, Costa Rica, the Dominican Republic, Ecuador, Paraguay, Brazil and Honduras.

Bikes Not Bombs

59 Amory, #103A
Roxbury , MA 02119
Tel: (617) 442-0004
email: bnbrox@igc.apc.org

Bikes Not Bombs (BNB) is a nonprofit, grassroots, development and solidarity organization that helps local groups form ecologically viable bicycle workshops and related projects in Central America, Haiti and in the U.S. These projects have involved the collecting of over 12,000 donated bicycles and tons of parts from across the U.S., recycling them to Nicaragua, Haiti, and recently to U.S. inner city youth programs. BNB provides technical assistance, training, tools, and financing for these projects and funds a bicycle-purchaser-revolving-loan-fund for campesinos in Nicaragua. Experienced, bilingual mechanics and personnel are placed to carry out field work.

Brethren Volunteer Services

1451 Dundee Avenue
Elgin, IL 60120
Tel: (800) 323-8039   Fax: (847) 742-6103

This Christian service program advocates justice, serves basic human and environmental needs, and supports peacemaking. Brethren Volunteer Services (BVS) places volunteers with locally sponsored church projects in Latin America, the Caribbean, the Middle East, and Europe. Positions abroad last 2 years and begin with a 3-week orientation in the U.S. BVS also has 1-year programs in the U.S. and China. In these programs volunteers are involved in a variety of community services including education, health care, office/secretarial work, and construction work. Volunteers can also participate in ministry to children, youth, senior citizens, homeless people, victims of domestic violence, prisoners, refugees, persons with AIDS, and others. Some positions require knowledge of a foreign language prior to orientation. Other requirements for special skills vary with assignment. Volunteers need not be Brethren or Christian, but must have an interest in examining the Christian faith. A college degree or equivalent life experience is required for overseas assignments. Travel expenses, room and board, medical coverage, and a monthly stipend of approximately $45 are provided.

Committee for Health Rights in the Americas (CHRIA)

(See listing under U.S. Voluntary Service Organizations.)

CONCERN/America

2024 North Broadway, #104
P.O. Box 1790
Santa Ana, CA 92702
Tel: (714) 953-8575   Fax: (714) 953-1242

CONCERN/America is an international development and refugee aid organization. CONCERN/America's main objective is to provide training, technical assistance, and material support to community-based programs in Third World countries and refugee camps. CONCERN/America volunteers serve for at least 1 year, and are professionals such as physicians, nurses, nutritionists, community organizers, public health and sanitation specialists. The focus of the work is on training local people to carry on programs that include health care training, developing nutrition and sanitation projects, organizing community development and income-generating projects, and conducting literacy campaigns. CONCERN/America volunteers currently serve in Bangladesh, El Salvador, Honduras, Guatemala, Mexico, and Sierra Leone. Volunteers must be at least 21 and fluent in Spanish. CONCERN/America provides transportation, room and board, health insurance, and a small stipend. In addition, a repatriation allowance of $50 per month of service is provided to the volunteer upon completion of contract.

Cristianos por la Paz en El Salvador (CRISPAZ)
Christian Volunteer Ministries
1135 Mission Road
San Antonio, TX 78210
Tel: (210) 534-6996   Fax: (210) 534-4995
email: crispaz@igc.apc.org

Volunteers work for a minimum of 1 year with responsibilities in 1 or more community programs. Placements include, but are not limited to, teaching, agriculture, health care, and pastoral ministries. Volunteers must have a sponsoring community that provides a monthly stipend and all other material needs. Volunteers must speak Spanish and have skills relevant to the assignment.

Doctors Without Borders USA, Inc.
11 East 26th Street, Suite 1904
New York, NY 10010
Tel: (212) 679-6800   Fax: (212) 679-7016

Doctors Without Borders/Medicins Sans Frontieres (MSF) is an independent, private medical relief organization. MSF volunteers observe strict medical ethics and assist victims of wars and natural disasters regardless of religious, political or economic influences. Every year 20 offices around the world recruit volunteers for 3,000 departures in up to 70 countries, over 20 of which are in a state of war and 11 of which are long term projects. The organization recruits members of the medical profession. All medical and paramedical specializations are represented. Specific operations often call for additional training in tropical medicine. Professional experience and foreign languages are also required. Contact the organization for more information and application materials.

Foundation for Sustainable Development
P.O. Box 37
Carrboro, NC 27510
(919) 932-5975   Fax (919) 932-7597

The Foundation for Sustainable Development is a private, non-profit organization dedicated to providing economic alternatives to students and adults who want hands-on development experience in Latin America. Projects focus on a range of areas including: sustainable agriculture, community development, environmental research and conservation and education. Programs are located in Mexico, Guatemala, and Nicaragua. Program lengths begin at one month and vary in length. Costs range from $650 to $1,650.

Fourth World Movement
7600 Willow Hill Drive
Landover, MD 20785-4658
Tel: (301) 336-9489   Fax: (301) 336-0092
email: fourthworldmovement@his.com

Fourth World Movement's work is based on three priorities: learning from the most disadvantaged families, understanding how they become trapped in persistent poverty, and planning and developing projects with them. Volunteers must first participate in a 2-month internship, living and working with full-time volunteers at the New York and Washington, D.C. area centers. Interns learn about the Movement and its approach to persistent poverty through their work, and through videos, readings, and discussion. Interns contribute toward food costs and receive a small weekly stipend after the first month. At the end of the internship, interns discuss with their supervisor what their 2-year assignment will be. Placement is made according to both the intern's interests and the Movement's needs. There are currently teams in 24 countries.

U.S. summer workcamps are also available at the international center in France. Workcamp volunteers are age 18 and older and participate in a 14-day program where they learn about poverty and do various kinds of manual work.

Frontiers Foundation Inc./Operation Beaver
2615 Danforth Avenue, Suite 203
Toronto, Ontario CANADA M4C 1L6
Tel: (416) 690-3930   Fax: (416) 690-3934

Frontiers Foundation is a community development service organization that works in partnership with communities in low-income, rural areas across northern Canada. These locally initiated projects build and improve housing, conduct training programs, and organize recreational activities in developing regions. Volunteers must be 18 or older and be available for a minimum of 12 weeks. Skills in carpentry, electrical work, and plumbing are preferred for construction projects; previous social service and experience with children are preferred for recreation projects. Projects run year round, but new volunteers begin in April and November. Accommodation, food, and travel inside Canada are provided. Placements of up to 18 months are possible provided the volunteer's work is satisfactory after the initial 12-week period.

Frontier Internship in Mission
International Coordinating Office
Ecumenical Centre, P.O. Box 2100
150, route de Ferney
1211 Geneva 2, SWITZERLAND
Tel: (22) 798 89 87   Fax: (22) 791 03 61
Telex: 23 423 OIK CH

Frontier Internship in Mission (FIM) is an international ecumenical program that provides people between 20 and 35 years of age with the opportunity to work abroad on social and theological issues for 2 years. Interns throughout the world are sent from an organization in their own country to work with one based in another nation. A relationship between the two organizations is developed through the intern who works on 1 of 3 frontier issue areas: economic injustice, resurgence of religion, and the juxtaposition of cultures. This study is followed by a year of re-integration work when the intern returns home. Travel costs and a subsistence allowance are paid by the coordinating office.

Habitat for Humanity International
121 Habitat Street
Americus, GA 31709
Tel: (912) 924-6935   Fax: (912) 924-6541

Habitat for Humanity International (HFHI) is a housing ministry helping poor people improve their living conditions worldwide.

Habitat places volunteers for 3-year periods in Africa, Asia, Latin America, and the Pacific Islands. Volunteers work on the organization, construction, and management of HFHI housing projects. Volunteers must be 21 or older. They receive housing, health insurance, payment of travel expenses, and a monthly stipend.

Construction and office-related work is also available in over 1,000 affiliates in the U.S. and in the International Headquarters in Americus, Georgia. Volunteers at the headquarters must be 18 years or older. They receive training, free housing and a $40 weekly stipend.

Heifer Project International
P.O. Box 808
Little Rock, AR 72203
Tel: (800) 422-1131

Heifer Project International (HPI) is a worldwide self-help organization that provides poultry and livestock, as well as training and related agricultural service, to farmers in developing areas in both the U.S. and the Third World. The program offers volunteer opportunities at its International Learning and Livestock Center and at its national office in Arkansas. HPI also conducts 8 to 10 day workcamp tours in countries around the world. Groups help build facilities for HPI projects and learn about development issues through rural village life. Volunteers pay their own expenses, which usually range from $1,000 to $3,000.

Institute for International Cooperation and Development
P.O. Box 103-APC
Williamstown, MA 01267
Tel: (413) 458-9828   Fax: (413) 458-3323

Institute for International Cooperation and Development (IICD) organizes travel, study, and solidarity courses in Africa and Latin America. Volunteers work in the following projects: Mozambique, tree-planting/community work; Zimbabwe, teaching in a literacy campaign and at a vocational school for disadvantaged youth and families; Nicaragua and Brazil, community construction work. Programs are 5-18 months long, including preparation and follow-up periods in the U.S. Preparation entails language, regional studies, practical training and fundraising. The follow-up period includes giving presentations and creating educational materials about the region visited. Costs vary depending on the program. It covers training, room and board, international insurance and airfare. The program is open for anyone 18 or older.

Institute of Cultural Affairs (ICA)
4220 North 25th Street
Phoenix, AZ 85016
Tel: (602) 955-4811 or (800) 742-4032   Fax: (602) 954-0563
or
ICA
4750 North Sheridan Road
Chicago, IL 60640
Tel: (312) 769-6363
or
ICA-West
1504 25th Avenue
Seattle, WA 98122
Tel: (206) 323-2100

The Institute of Cultural Affairs (ICA) is an international development organization with offices in 29 countries. Each ICA office is in contact with ICA offices in other countries and can provide information on opportunities for volunteers. Volunteers have recently worked on community development projects in Rio de Janero and on the Ivory Coast. The Portugal office offers 2-week workcamps in their Montemure Mountain project. For information, contact their office nearest to you.

(Also see listing under U.S. Voluntary Service Organizations.)

Interplast

300-B Pioneer Way
Mountain View , CA 94041
Tel: (415) 962-0123   Fax: (415) 962-1619

Interplast sends medical volunteers to perform reconstructive surgery to Ecuador, Argentina, Brazil, Peru, Chile, Honduras, El Salvador, Nicaragua, Mexico, Bangladesh, Myanmar, Mongolia, Vietnam, Thailand, Jamaica and Nepal. Positions include plastic surgeons, anesthesiologists, operating-room nurses, pediatricians, and recovery nurses. Placements are for 2 weeks. Spanish is desirable for Central and South American assignments, but not required. Physicians are encouraged to pay their own travel expenses; room and board are provided.

MADRE / Sisters Without Borders

121 West 27th Street, Room 301
New York, NY 10001
Tel: (212) 627-0444   Fax: (212) 675-3704

MADRE places women professionals trained in midwifery, obstetrics, nutrition, sexually transmitted disease training, drug counseling, anti-violence training, herbal medicine and stress counseling in Nicaragua, El Salvador, and Guatemala. Volunteers provide service and conduct training. Sisters Without Borders, a gender based health exchange program, is a critical part of MADRE's work. In short term residences volunteers exchange skills and information with counselors and health providers through work with women and children in Nicaragua, El Salvador and Guatemala. Volunteers must have credentials and experience in the field in which they would like to work. Spanish is required. Volunteers cover their own costs for travel expenses and accommodations. Residencies last approximately one to two weeks.

Maryknoll Mission Association of the Faithful

P.O. Box 307
Maryknoll, NY 10545
Tel: (914) 762-6364   Fax: (914) 762-7031

Maryknoll lay missioners serve for 3 years in Asia, Africa, or Latin America. Opportunities include community organizing, health education, teaching, adult education, human rights, and pastoral team ministry. All new lay missioners attend a 4-month orientation at Maryknoll, New York prior to their overseas assignment. Language training is available in the country of assignment. Applicants must have a college degree or skill, plus a minimum of 1 year experience after completion of formal education. Applicants must also be Roman Catholic. Travel expenses, room, board, health insurance, and stipend are paid by Maryknoll.

Mennonite Central Committee

21 South 12th Street
Akron, PA 17501-0500
Tel: (717) 859-1151   Fax: (717) 859-2171

Mennonite Central Committee (MCC) is the development and relief agency of the Mennonite and Brethren in Christ churches. Currently more than 900 persons serve in agriculture, health, education, social services, and community development fields in more than 50 countries, including the U.S. and Canada. Qualifications depend on assignment. Transportation, living expenses, and a small stipend are provided. MCC asks that volunteers be Christian, actively involved in a church congregation, and in agreement with its nonviolent principles. Placements are for 3 years overseas, 2 years in North America.

Mission Volunteers/Overseas
Mission Volunteers/USA
Presbyterian Church (USA)
100 Witherspoon Street, Rm 3409
Louisville, KY 40202-1396
Tel: 1-800-779-6779   Fax: (502) 569-5975

The Mission Services Recruitment Office helps church-supported organizations and projects find full-time volunteers both within the U.S. and overseas. International assignments usually involve teaching or health care in Africa, Asia, or the Middle East. Volunteers must be church affiliated. Length of service can be from three months to two years. Room and board are provided.

National FFA Organization
Student Services - International
P.O. Box 15160
Alexandria, VA 22309-0160
Tel: (703) 360-3600   Fax: (703) 360-5524

The National FFA Organization (formerly known as Future Farmers of America) offers the World Experience in Agriculture program which provides a cross-cultural experience combined with a practical, hands-on agricultural program. Participants, usually age 18-24, observe, study and participate in the agricultural operation of a host family they choose to visit. In exchange for the assistance provided at the host placement, participants usually receive room and board and a monthly stipend. Previous experience in agriculture is helpful and a strong interest in learning about agriculture is essential. Applicants must provide adequate recommendations from past employers and instructors and be prepared to study and learn a new language if placed in a non-English speaking country. Placements are available in over 20 countries for three, six or 12 months. Program fees range from $1500 to $6000 depending on the country and length of stay. Fees include international airfare, a two-day orientation, visa fee (if required), host arrangements and health and accident insurance. Applications and program brochures are available upon request.

Nicaragua Center for Community Action (NICCA)
2140 Shattuck Avenue, Box 2063
Berkeley, CA 94704
Tel: (510) 832-4959

Nicaragua Center for Community Action (NICCA) sends work brigades of 10 to 20 people to Nicaragua to work on sustainable agriculture projects. The group works side-by-side with Nicaraguans, rebuilding their economy and continuing support for their revolution. Brigadistas live with a family on their cooperative and share firsthand the Nicaraguans' struggles in the face of the resistance from the Chamorro government. The cost is $500 and airfare which includes all expenses plus airfare from San Francisco.

The Partnership for Service-Learning
815 Second Avenue, Suite 315
New York, NY 10017
Tel: (212) 986-0989   Fax: (212) 986-5039
email: pslny@ad.com

The Partnership's programs combine formal learning with extensive community service to those in need. The programs are available in: Czech Republic, Ecuador, England, France, India, Israel, Jamaica, Mexico, the Philippines, Scotland and South Dakota. A variety of community service projects in each location include: children, teaching, handicapped, literacy, community development, recreation and women's issues. Program periods are summer, fall/spring, two terms in January intersession. Costs vary, but begin at $6,500 for a two-term program to the Philippines. Most applicants are undergraduates, but anyone may apply. The Partnership Service-Learning objective is to move beyond preconceptions to encounter the realities of another culture.

Pastors for Peace

610 West 28th Street
Minneapolis, MN 55408
Tel: (612) 870-7121   Fax: (612) 870-7109

Pastors for Peace is an ecumenical project based in the religious community and includes activists from all sectors of society. Anyone who works for peace with justice is a "pastor" for peace. Pastors for Peace organizes humanitarian aid caravans, work brigades and delegations to Mexico, Central America and Cuba. Cost ranges from $550 to $1150 depending on the project. Anyone is eligible, however children under 18 years of age must be accompanied by a parent or guardian. Call Pastors for Peace for more information and applications.

Peace Brigades International

2642 College Ave
Berkeley CA 94704
Tel: (510) 540-0749   Tel/Fax: (510) 849-1247
email: pbiusa@igc.apc.org

Peace Brigades International's (PBI) Central America Project sends nonviolent/nonpartisan teams to Guatemala to monitor human rights violations. International volunteers accompany threatened individuals, give workshops in peace education (mediation, human rights, conflict resolution, etc.), and upon their return, conduct public education programs through speaking tours. Volunteers should be 25 years or older, fluent in Spanish, and able to make a commitment to work a minimum of 7 months. Volunteers must also undergo training in nonviolence before being accepted. Volunteers pay transportation and health insurance; other costs are paid by PBI.

PBI's projects in Sri Lanka, Colombia, North America, Haiti, and the Balkans are similar to the Central America Project in their goals. Volunteers must be at least 25 years old and able to make a commitment of 7 months. Language requirements are: English

(Sri Lanka and North America), Spanish (Colombia), or French (Haiti and North America). PBI training must also be undertaken before being accepted to work in these projects.

(Also see listing under U.S. Voluntary Service Organizations.)

Peacework

305 Washington Street, SW
Blacksburg, VA 24060-4745
Tel: (800) 272-5519   Fax: (540) 552-0119

Peacework/Latin America
3731 First Ave.
San Diego, CA 92103
Tel: (619) 299-9763   Fax: (619) 291-5616

Peacework sponsors volunteer work projects in developing communities around the world. Volunteers from different countries and cultures come together to participate in a common learning and service program. Orientation and cultural experiences are included along with general work on housing, schools and clinics. Leadership and planning is provided by the host community. Volunteers are typically college age or recent graduates, but programs are open to all ages. Projects change from year to year and have been offered in Mexico, Ghana, Russia, Cuba, the United States, Nicaragua and Palestine. Typical costs range from $500 to $800 plus airfare. Limited scholarships are available.

Plenty USA

P.O. Box 394
Summertown, TN 38483 USA
Tel/Fax (615) 964-4864
email: plentyusa@MCIMAIL.com

Founded in 1974, Plenty works around the world helping disadvantaged communities achieve self-sufficiency in food production, primary health care, energy, communications, small business enterprises, and other appropriate village-scale technologies. Special focus is on indigenous communities and the environment. Volunteers pay their own travel and living expenses. No special requirements or language skills required for most projects. Short and long term volunteer opportunities are available. Send a SASE for more information and application materials.

Service Civil International
c/o Innisfree Village
5474 Walnut Level Road
Crozet, VA 22932
Tel: (804) 823-1826

Service Civil International (SCI) organizes workcamps in the U.S., Europe, Asia, and Africa to promote cross-cultural understanding and international peace. Volunteers work on environmental, construction, solidarity, and social service projects and live together in simple quarters for 2 to 3 weeks. Volunteers must be 16 or older for U.S. workcamps, 18 or older for European camps, and at least 21, with SCI workcamp experience, for a project in Africa or Asia. Volunteers pay travel expenses and a small fee; SCI covers room, board, and accident insurance. Many workcamps are accessible to disabled people.

The Training Exchange
The Training Exchange is now part of CHRIA

United Nations Volunteers
Palais des Nations
CH-1211 Geneva 10
SWITZERLAND
Tel: (41 22) 788-2455   Fax: (41 22) 788-2501
Email: udp090   Internet: Enquires @ unv.ch

United Nations Volunteers
1990 K Street NW, 8th Floor
Washington, DC 20526
(202) 606-3370 or (800) 424-8580 X 2243   Fax: (202) 606-3024

United Nations Volunteers (UNV) assigns qualified and experienced women and men to development; facilitation of community-based development initiatives; humanitarian relief; and peace operations, democracy and human rights operations of the United Nations. Some 4,000 UNVs, average age nearly 40, drawn from 124 nations served nearly 130 countries in the course of 1994, in projects executed by governments, UN agencies or by UNV itself. Development assignments are normally for two years, but the duration can be less in the humanitarian relief, peace operations, democracy and human rights operations areas. U.S. candidates should apply via the Peace Corps, specifying UNV. Essential requirements include graduate/postgraduate degrees or equivalent technical qualifications and several years' working experience. Women and retirees are particularly welcome. A monthly living allowance, housing, health insurance, return air fare, and a modest resettlement allowance are provided.

Visions in Action
3637 Fulton Street, NW
Washington, D.C. 20007
Tel: (202) 625-7403

Visions in Action arranges for volunteers to work in urban areas of Africa and the Caribbean with development organizations and the media. Placements are made for 1 year in Kenya, Uganda, Tanzania, Somalia, Zimbabwe, and Burkina Faso, the Dominican Republic, and for six or twelve months in South Africa or Mexico. Placements include project management, health care, journalism, youth-group organizing, research and writing, human rights, democracy, housing, and community development. All participants take part in a one-month orientation that includes intensive language training, cross-cultural awareness, and field trips to development projects. An additional purpose of the program is to educate people in the U.S. about Third World countries through volunteers' published articles and slide show or videotape presentations given to schools and groups upon return to the U.S. Most volunteers live in group houses with other volunteers. Volunteers pay for their own expenses which average $4,500 to $6,000, including airfare. All volunteers receive a small monthly stipend.

Voluntarios Solidarios

Task Force on Latin American and the Caribbean
515 Broadway
Santa Cruz, CA 95060
Tel: (408) 423-1626   Fax: (408) 423-8716

Voluntarios Solidarios works with organizations in Latin America and the Caribbean engaged in nonviolence education, human rights documentation, and advocacy efforts with the region's poor majority. Each volunteer's work is shaped by the needs of the host organization. Projects include: technical assistance in skills ranging from carpentry to computer operation to recycling; translation of publications; collaboration in work with children, peasants and women; sharing methodologies in popular education and conflict resolution. Volunteers need to be 21 or older. Placements are from 3 months to 2 years. Volunteers are responsible for providing their own costs including travel to and from the region, food, lodging and personal expenses.

Volunteers for Peace, Inc.

43 Tiffany Road
Belmont, VT 05730
Tel: (802) 259-2759   Fax: (802) 259-2922
email: vfp@vermontel.com

Volunteers for Peace (VFP) serves as an information and referral center for international opportunities to support community projects. VFP also coordinates workcamps throughout the world. In these 2 to 3 week workcamps 20 people from 4 or more countries join together to work on community development projects in the fields of construction, restoration, the environment, social services, agriculture and archaeology. Volunteers pay an administration fee of $175 per camp which includes room, board and sometimes accident insurance. Call or write for free newsletter.

Volunteers in Asia
P.O. Box 4543
Stanford, CA 94309
Tel: (415) 723-3228

At the request of Asian institutions, Volunteers in Asia (VIA) places undergraduates and recent graduates in teaching and English resource positions in Taiwan, China, Indonesia, Thailand, Laos and Vietnam. Applicants must reside in the Santa Cruz or San Francisco Bay Area 1 year prior to overseas placement and must attend a 3 and a half month, part-time preparation and training program at Stanford University. Volunteers pay an initial fee of $1,500 for a 1-year placement or $950 for a 2-year placement. This fee covers insurance, training costs, and round-trip airfare. The host institution provides an in-country stipend for basic living expenses.

Volunteers in Mission
4503 Broadway
San Antonio, TX 78209
Tel: (210) 828-2224   Fax: (210) 828-9741
Principal Contact: Karen Gosetti

VIM seeks a new economic, social and political order that promotes justice and solidarity. Volunteers work with homeless women and children, do pastoral work, teach in U.S./Mexico border schools and in the Sierra Tarahumara, and provide preventive health care. Programs are organized in both the U.S. and

Mexico. Volunteers must be at least 21 years old; single or married with no dependents; commit to one year in the U.S. or two to three years in Mexico; and if volunteering in Mexico, be Catholic. Volunteers pay cost of transportation to the orientation site and language school if needed. All other costs are paid by VIM.

Volunteers in Overseas Cooperative Assistance

50 F Street NW, Suite 1075
Washington, D.C. 20001
Tel: (800) 929-8622   Fax: (202) 783-7204
Telex: 6974812 VOCA

Volunteers in Overseas Cooperative Assistance (VOCA) sends experienced professionals in cooperative development, agriculture, and agribusiness to Third World countries and emerging democracies. VOCA volunteers work in Africa, Asia, the Near East, Latin America and the Caribbean, as well as in emerging democracies in Central and Eastern Europe, the Baltics and the former Soviet republics (including Kazakhstan, Russia, and Ukraine). Volunteers provide short-term technical assistance to cooperatives (rural electrification, credit unions, and agriculture) and to private or governmental agricultural organizations. Projects usually run from 1 to 3 months. Volunteers are generally retired cooperative executives, university professors, and highly experienced agriculturalists. VOCA pays all expenses and includes spouses on assignments over 1 month.

Volunteers Workcamp Association of Ghana/VOLU

P.O. Box 1540
Accra, GHANA
Tel: 663486

VOLU, one of Africa's oldest and largest workcamp agencies, recruits volunteers from Europe, the U.S., and countries around Africa (including Ghana itself) to work on projects such as building schools and roads, planting trees, etc., during the summer and winter holidays. No special skills are required. Volunteers are asked to pay $100 to cover room and board costs, plus their own travel expenses. Camps usually last 3 weeks, and volunteers may participate in more than one.

Witness for Peace
110 Maryland Ave. NE, Suite #304
Washington, D.C. 20002
Tel: (202) 544-0781   Fax: (202) 544-1187
email: witness@igc.apc.org

Volunteers with Witness for Peace (WFP), a faith-based organization, work with communities throughout Nicaragua, Guatemala, and Haiti, making a 2-year commitment. Long-term volunteers serve a variety of purposes, including documenting human rights abuses, studying the effects of United States foreign and economic policies on the region, providing socio-political analyses of domestic affairs, facilitating short-term delegations of US citizens, and most importantly, standing with the people in the spirit of international awareness and the ethos of nonviolence as a means for positive social change. Volunteers must be U.S. citizens, at least 21 years old, and fluent in Spanish and/or Creole. Volunteers pay costs of round-trip air fare and raise $1,000 for WFP to help cover living expenses. WFP provides training, room and board, medical, and a monthly stipend.

WorldTeach, Inc.
Harvard Institute for International Development
One Eliot Street
Cambridge, MA 02138-5705
Tel: 1-800-4-TEACH-0   Fax : (617) 495-1599
email: worldteach@hiid.harvard.edu

WorldTeach, Inc., a non-profit program based at Harvard University, sends volunteers as teachers to developing countries that have requested assistance. WorldTeach currently works in Costa

Rica, Ecuador, Namibia, South Africa, Russia, Poland, Thailand and China. Volunteers teach at all levels of education including primary schools and universities. Volunteers pay a fee that covers the cost of airfare, health insurance, training, placement, field support and administration ($3,600-$4,550). The host school, community, or government provides either room and board or housing and a modest living allowance (anywhere from $50 to $300/month). Programs in Costa Rica, Ecuador, Namibia, South Africa, Russia, Poland, and Thailand last for one year and require a bachelor's degree. The Shanghai Summer Teaching Program (SSTP), in China, lasts for eight weeks and is open to undergraduates. SSTP volunteers combine teaching English to Chinese high school students with studying Chinese.

U.S. VOLUNTARY
SERVICE ORGANIZATIONS

Working overseas is not the only way to gain community development experience. In many areas of the U.S. people face conditions of poverty similar to those found in the Third World. Voluntary service in the U.S. can offer a low-cost opportunity for building solid credentials towards a career in community development.

Abya Yala Fund
P.O. Box 28386
Oakland, CA 94604
(510) 763-6553
email: abyayala@ipc.apc.org

Abya Yala is an organization providing resources and technical training to indigenous people from South and Central America and Mexico. The group works to help indigenous peoples address development issues in their communities in a way that is culturally appropriate and environmentally sustainable. Interns will work at the Oakland office on research, administration, fundraising, event coordination, and translation. Plans for opening regional offices in Central and South America will open opportunities for overseas volunteer work. Preferably interns speak Spanish, Portuguese, or an indigenous language.

ACORN
117 Harrison, #200
Chicago, IL 60605
Tel: (312)939-7488   Fax: (312)939-8256

ACORN (Association of Community Organizations for Reform Now) is a neighborhood-based, multi-racial membership organization of low-income families working to gain power within institutions that

affect their everyday lives. Volunteers work as grassroots organizers throughout the U.S. They receive a salary and must commit to
1 year of service. A working knowledge of Spanish and previous
organizing experience are preferred, but not required.

Bike-Aid

Overseas Development Network (ODN)
333 Valencia Street, Suite 330
San Francisco, CA 94103
Tel: (415) 431-4480 or (800) RIDE-808
email: odn@igc.apc.org
world wide web http:\\www.igc.apc.org\odn\

Bike-Aid is an educational and fundraising project of the Overseas Development Network (ODN), a national student-based
organization which addresses the global problems of poverty and
injustice by raising money for small-scale, self-help community
development projects in both the U.S. and the Third World. ODN
also organizes educational events in the U.S. Each summer six
Bike-Aid teams of 20 cyclists set off from Seattle, Portland, San
Francisco, Montreal and Chapel Hill, NC to bike across the country, finally joining together in Washington, D.C. Along the way
cyclists meet with community activists in homeless shelters,
farmers' cooperatives, environmental action groups and Native
American communities. Bike-Aid participants both educate people about the work of ODN and learn about the issues facing the
communities they visit.

Bikes Not Bombs

(See listing under International Voluntary Service
Organizations.)

Brethren Volunteer Services

(See listing under International Voluntary Service
Organizations.)

Center for Third World Organizing

1218 East 21st Street
Oakland, CA 94606
Tel: (510) 533-7583   Fax: (510) 533-0923

Center for Third World Organizing (CTWO) is a research and training center working on issues affecting Third World communities in the U.S. Their summer apprenticeship program for minority activists provides training and field experience for young people of color who are involved in work for social change. Each summer this 3-month program trains people, primarily college students, in the techniques of community organizing. Volunteers for this program receive housing and a stipend. Other internships are sometimes available, including research and writing for the Center newsletter.

Citizen Action

1730 Rhode Island Ave. N.W., #403
Washington, D.C. 20036
Tel: (202) 775-1580

Citizen Action is a national membership organization of people working for social change. There are over 32 state affiliate offices throughout the country. Volunteers work as field organizers and fundraisers around issues such as health care, the environment, foreign policy, energy, and insurance reform. Excellent verbal communication and good interpersonal skills, as well as commitment to progressive issues are required. Placements vary from 6 months to a year. Stipends are negotiable.

Committee for Health Rights In the Americas

474 Valencia Street, Suite 120
San Francisco, CA 94103
Tel: (415) 431-7760
Fax: (415)431-7768
email: chria@igc.apc.org

Committee for Health Rights In the Americas (CHRIA) is a non-profit humanitarian organization working in support of health rights across borders. CHRIA works on behalf of immigrant and refugee health rights and has projects in El Salvador, Nicaragua, Guatemala, and Mexico. Spanish-speaking mental health professionals are needed to staff the Centro Ignacio Martín-Baró in Berkeley, California, a volunteer mental health clinic primarily for Central American refugees. CHRIA administers the Training Exchange, a project which sends health care professionals who are fluent in Spanish to Central America to help develop primary care training programs in medical schools, nursing schools, and other health care institutions. CHRIA takes delegations to Central America and Mexico for technical exchange, medical aid, and documentation of health rights.

East Coast Migrant Health Project, Inc.

1234 Massachusetts Avenue, NW, #C-1017
Washington, D.C. 20005
Tel: (202) 347-7377   Fax: (202) 347-6385

The East Coast Migrant Health Project Inc., (ECMHP) directs its energies toward the empowerment of migratory and seasonal farmworkers and their families through the provisions of health care, outreach services, preventative health education, and group networking. ECMHP places staff with health providers along the U.S. East Coast to ensure that services are available and accessible to migrant/seasonal farmworkers. Volunteers are health professionals of all levels, as well as social workers and others interested in providing outreach services. There is a particular need for nurse practitioners, community and public health nurses, licensed practical nurses, and other professionals with specialty certificates. The project also recruits people in allied health fields, such as social workers, nutritionists, health educators, psychologists, and community service workers. Geographic mobility and possession of a car with adequate insurance is a must. Staff receive a competitive salary and benefits. The minimum length of commitment is one year. Language skills in Spanish, or Creole are helpful.

Fourth World Movement
(See listing under International Voluntary Service Organizations.)

Habitat for Humanity International
(See listing under International Voluntary Service Organizations.)

Heifer Project International
(See listing under International Voluntary Service Organizations.)

Human Service Alliance
3983 Old Greensboro Rd.
Winston-Salem, NC 27101
(910) 761-8745   Fax: (910) 722-7882
email: 72632.1002@compuserve.com

Human Service Alliance is a volunteer nonprofit service organization in suburban North Carolina. There are no charges for any services offered. Two of its primary project areas are care for the terminally ill (24-hour care on-site), and care for developmentally disabled children on weekends in Respite Care. Community live-in volunteers from around the world cook and serve food for residents, and care for the building. Room, board and training provided. Volunteers need to provide their own transportation. Full-time, live-in volunteers serve 50-60 hours per week with one day off. Length of stay varies from two weeks to a year or longer. No age requirement.

Institute of Cultural Affairs (ICA)
4220 North 25th Street
Phoenix, AZ 85016
Tel: (602) 955-4811 or (800) 742-4032   Fax: (602) 954-0563
or
ICA
4750 North Sheridan Road
Chicago, IL 60640
Tel: (312) 769-6363
or
ICA-West
1504 25th Avenue
Seattle, WA 98122
Tel: (206) 323-2100

The Institute of Cultural Affairs (ICA) is a non-profit research, training, and demonstration group concerned with developing leadership capacities and global awareness. The Phoenix office of ICA needs interns and volunteers for office work, community development, educational research, and graphics production. The Chicago office offers a 3-week training course for those interested in human development, team building and strategic planning along with service career exploration. In Seattle, volunteers can work on "Rite of Passage Journeys" for youths and other community development projects. For information on ICA projects, contact the office nearest you.

(Also see listing under International Voluntary Service Organizations.)

Jesuit Volunteer Corps
P.O. Box 3266
Berkeley, CA 94703
Tel: (510) 653-8564

Jesuit Volunteer Corps (JVC) places volunteers throughout the U.S. for 1 year to work with poor and marginalized people. They serve as teachers, nurses, counselors and social workers. Projects are defined by local need. Volunteers live modestly in a cooperative household with other JVC volunteers. The host organization provides room and board, travel expenses at year's end, health insurance and a $75 monthly stipend. Volunteers are usually at least 21 years old, have a college degree, and are motivated by Christian principles.

Los Niños
287 "G" Street
Chula Vista, CA 91910
Tel: (619) 426-9110   Fax: (619) 426-6664

Los Niños provides long-term community development programs along the U.S.-Mexico border in the areas of agriculture and nutrition. The programs are designed to promote self-reliance and social awareness. Long-term development projects are carried out by interns serving 1-year placements. They receive room, board, and a $50 per month stipend. Summer, weekend, and weeklong programs are also offered to U.S. participants who want to learn more about development along the U.S.-Mexico border.

Lutheran Volunteer Corps
1226 Vermont Avenue, NW
Washington, D.C. 20005
Tel: (202) 387-3222

Lutheran Volunteer Corps volunteers work through agencies in a number of areas including direct service, public policy, advocacy, community organizing, and education. Placements are in Baltimore, MD; Wilmington, DE; Washington, D.C.; Chicago, IL; Milwaukee, WI; Minneapolis/St. Paul, MN, Seattle and Tacoma, WA. Volunteers live communally with 3 to 7 other volunteers. Travel, room and board, medical coverage, and daily work-related transportation expenses are covered. The program is open to people from all faith perspectives.

Marianist Voluntary Service Community
P.O. Box 9224
Wright Brothers Branch
Dayton, OH 45409
Tel: (513) 229-4630 or (513) 229-3287

Volunteers are placed for 1 year in urban areas in Kentucky, New York, and Ohio. Placements include social work and community organizing, educational opportunities, health care, and housing rehabilitation. Volunteers must be at least 20 years of age, possess skills appropriate to placement, and be able to pay transportation expenses to and from the city. The organization provides a stipend. Volunteers must be willing to live communally, sharing household responsibilities, expenses, meals and group prayer.

Mennonite Central Committee
(See listing under International Voluntary Service Organizations.)

Mennonite Voluntary Service
722 Main Street
P.O. Box 347
Newton, KS 67114-0347
Tel: (316) 283-5100

Mennonite Voluntary Service (MVS) helps meet the needs of poor and disadvantaged people in the U.S. and Canada. Volunteer placements range from staffing food banks and emergency assistance centers to working with migrant farmworkers. Social work, community organization, housing rehabilitation, and education skills are in particular demand. Initial terms of 2 years are strongly encouraged, though some assignments are available for 1 year. Spanish is helpful or required for some positions. Volunteers must be Christian and at least 18 years old. All expenses are covered by MVS.

Mission Volunteers/USA
(See listing under International Voluntary Service Organizations.)

Passionist Lay Missioners
5700 North Harlem Avenue
Chicago, IL 60631-2342
Tel: (312) 631-6336   Fax: (312) 631-8059

Passionist Lay Missioners are volunteers who seek to address immediate and systemic problems of poverty by working with economically disadvantaged and disenfranchised people in Chicago, Detroit, and Cincinnati. Positions begin in August and last for 1 year or more and include social workers, youth workers, advocates for the homeless, teachers and teacher's aides, emergency intervention workers, community organizers, peace and justice advocates, prisoners' rights advocates, child care workers, counselors, domestic violence workers, clerical workers, care givers for the elderly, legal aides, and more. Volunteers live in community in low income, inner-city neighborhoods. They live a simple lifestyle and explore connections between work, community, faith and social justice. Volunteers pay for their own transportation to the orientation in August. Room and board, health insurance, monthly stipend of $100 and transportation during the year are provided. Applicants must be 21 years old, with some college education or practical work experience, and be willing to engage in spiritual reflection.

Peace Brigades International - North America Project
Box 1233, Harvard Square Station
Cambridge, MA 02238
Tel: (617) 491-4226

Peace Brigades International (PBI) has recently formed a North America Project (NAP) based on the model of work done by PBI in Central America and Sri Lanka. The goal is to help bring about a just resolution of conflict without resorting to violence. The initial focus of NAP is the struggle for justice by Native Americans, but the project is not necessarily limited to this area.

PBI will form international teams of volunteers who will seek the most appropriate ways to support nonviolent struggle for justice in each situation. Some ways might include trainings for local people doing human rights watches, observing, accompanying people who might be threatened for their social activism, peace education, and developing a network of people who will respond with letters, faxes, and phone calls to appropriate authorities in cases of urgency. NAP volunteers may also be formed into on-call "Ready Response Brigades," that will be ready to respond in a crisis situation on short notice.

Potential volunteers must speak English, be at least 25 years old, and attend a 1 to 2 week PBI training.

(Also see listing under International Voluntary Service Organizations)

Plenty USA
(See listing under International Voluntary Service Organizations.)

Proyecto Libertad
113 North 1st Street
Harlingen, TX 78550
Tel: (210) 425-9552   (210) 425-8249

Proyecto Libertad (PL) is a legal office on the Texas-Mexico border representing Central American refugees. PL provides legal services, help in applying for political asylum, and advocacy for Central Americans (including minors) in detention. PL also raises bond money and contacts relatives. On a systemic level, PL participates in federal litigation to protect refugee rights. Volunteers work on all aspects of the program. Volunteers must speak Spanish and be sensitive to multicultural differences. A car is extremely useful. Volunteers cover their own expenses, but some assistance may be available.

Service Civil International
(See listing under International Voluntary Service Organizations.)

Sioux YMCAs
P.O. Box 218
Dupree, SD 57623
Tel: (605) 365-5232   Fax: (605) 365-5230

Volunteers of college age or older serve for two months during the summer as camp staff at Leslie Marrowbone Memorial YMCA Camp, working with eight- to fourteen-year-old Sioux children. Also needed are community work volunteers to live in small, isolated Lakota communities to support various youth and family projects. These placements are for nine months through Americorps. Other community volunteer positions are available. Volunteers must have camp or community work skills, and be flexible and able to share their own cultures, as well as relate to others. The YMCA can help with room and board.

Teach for America
20 Exchange Place, 8th floor
New York, NY 10005
Mailing address:
P.O. Box 5114
New York, NY 10185
Tel: (800) 832-1230 or (212) 425-9039   Fax: (212) 425-9347

Teach for America is a national teacher corps of individuals from all ethnic backgrounds and academic majors. Corps members work for a minimum of 2 years as full-time, salaried teachers in urban and rural under-resourced public schools. The summer prior to entering the classroom, participants attend an intensive training institute. The program is intended for recent college graduates who are interested in making a difference and having an immediate impact.

United Farm Workers

P.O. Box 62, La Paz
Keene, CA 93531
Tel: (805) 822-5571

United Farm Workers (UFW) works for justice for farm workers and safe food for consumers. Volunteers spend 1 year or more in rural or urban areas, organizing farm workers and consumers. Opportunities are also available in computer-related and administrative capacities. Volunteers receive room and board and a small stipend.

Ursuline Companions in Mission

College Center Room 155
New Rochelle, NY 10805
Tel: (914) 654-5270 or (914) 576-6774

Volunteers are sent to inner-city and rural work sites in the U.S. to provide education, social work, health care, pastoral ministry, and outreach to the elderly. Volunteers must be 21 years or older and possess skills compatible with needs of specific ministries. Placements are for summer or for year round.

Voices on the Border

P.O. Box 53081, Temple Heights Station
Washington, D.C. 20009
Tel: (202) 529-2912   Fax: (202) 529-0897
email: voices@igc.apc.org

Voices on the Border promotes sustainable, equitable community-based development and contracts between repatriated communities in Eastern El Salvador and partner communities and individuals in the United States. VOTB supports development projects and helps organize U.S. delegations to these communities. Delegations generally last for ten days and take place several times a year. Total cost for participating is approximately $1100.

Witness for Peace
(See listing under International Voluntary Service Organizations.)

ALTERNATIVE TRAVEL & STUDY OVERSEAS

A number of groups conduct "reality tours" in the Third World and the U.S. These are socially responsible educational tours that provide participants with firsthand experience of the political, economic, and social structures that create or sustain hunger, poverty, and environmental degradation. Tour participants meet with people from diverse sectors with various perspectives on issues of agriculture, development and the environment. They often stay with local people, visit rural areas, and meet with grassroots organizers. The experience and insights gained on such a tour may influence participants' future work for democratic social change.

Many universities offer study-abroad programs. This section mentions just a few of these.

African American Studies Program

19 South La Salle Street, #301
Chicago, IL 60603
Tel: (312) 443-0929

The African American Studies Program offers a variety of study tours throughout Africa. Past tour themes have included economic and political development of states and the role of women in the family. Tours are led by scholars of African studies.

Bicycle Africa

International Bicycle Fund
4887 Columbia Drive South, #Q
Seattle, WA 98108-1919
Tel/Fax: (206) 628-9314

The IBF arranges 2- to 4-week cultural and educational bicycle tours in Cameroon, Kenya, Uganda, Tanzania, Tunisia, West Africa, and Zimbabwe. Specialists accompany groups to areas seldom visited by Westerners. Cycling is moderate and participants do not need to have extensive touring experience. The costs range from $900 to $1,290, not including air fare. The International Bicycle Fund promotes bicycle transportation, economic development, international understanding and safety education.

Center for Global Education
Augsburg College
2211 Riverside Avenue
Minneapolis, MN 55454
Tel: (612) 330-1159   Fax: (612) 330-1695
email: globaled@augsburg.edu
http:\\augsberg.edu/global/

The Center for Global Education designs and coordinates travel seminars to Central America, Mexico, South America, the Asia-Pacific region, the Caribbean, Southern Africa, and the Middle East. The goal is to introduce participants to the reality of poverty and injustice in the Third World. Participants meet with a wide range of representatives in government and business, church and grassroots communities. Focus is on food and agriculture, human rights, women's roles, and the role and responsibility of the church in working for social change. The Center's programs are utilized by a wide variety of civic groups, churches, and individuals. They also arrange longer-term study programs in development.

Center for Responsible Tourism
P.O. Box 827
San Anselmo, CA 94979
Tel: (415) 258-6544   Fax: (415) 258-1608

The Center for Responsible Tourism is a nonprofit organization dedicated to justice in tourism. It coordinates a network of North American groups that share its values. The Center maintains a library, publishes a newsletter, hosts conferences and offers the services of a speakers' bureau in order to work towards changing North American travelers' attitudes to be compatible with a sustainable global society.

Co-op Travel-LInks America
120 Beacon Street
Somerville, MA 02143
Tel: (800) 648-2667 or in MA (617) 497-8163
Fax: (617) 492-3720

Travel-Links is a full-service travel agency that emphasizes responsible tourism and seeks to promote understanding and cooperation among people through non-exploitive travel.

Earthwatch
680 Mount Auburn Street
P.O. Box 403
Watertown, MA 02272-9924
Tel: (617) 926-8200   (617) 926-8532

Earthwatch sponsors scholarly field research using volunteers to help scientists on research expeditions around the world. Among these EarthCorps expeditions is a project, sponsored by the Institute for Food and Development Policy (Food First), that examines sustainable living and resource use in Kerala, India. Kerala, an Indian state with a per capita GNP of just $182 (compared to $17,480 in the U.S.) has both an adult literacy rate and a life expectancy that compare with those in the U.S. Each volunteer lives with a family, partaking in work, recreation, and all other daily community activities with the help of an English-speaking cultural guide. Three times a week, teams meet to discuss their experience of Keralan society. Projects last 1 month and cost $1,695. Airfare is additional.

f

Global Exchange
2017 Mission Street, Suite 303
San Francisco, CA 94110
Tel: (415) 255-7296
Fax: (415) 255-7498
email: globalexch@igc.org

Global Exchange organizes Reality Tours, Study Seminars and Human Rights Delegations to more than 25 countries. These study tours offer a unique opportunity to learn firsthand about pressing issues confronting the Third World. Tour participants meet with peasant and labor organizers, community and religious leaders, peace activists, environmentalists, scholars, students, indigenous leaders, and government officials. Trips are to South Africa, Zimbabwe, Cuba, Haiti, Mexico (Chiapas), Chile, Central America, Senegal, Vietnam, China, North Korea, Philippines, Northern Ireland, Ecuador, Mongolia, Nicaragua and Brazil. Costs range from $800 to $3200. Global Exchange also offers Spanish language programs in Mexico and Guatemala, and soon in Cuba, and opportunities for volunteer work in Mexico and Honduras. There are also volunteer opportunities at Global Exchange's San Francisco office.

Global Volunteers
375 E. Little Canada Road
St. Paul, MN 55117
Tel: (800) 487-1074   Fax: (612) 482-0915

Global Volunteers forms teams of 8 to 12 volunteers who live in host communities and work with villagers on development projects selected by local leadership. The projects may involve construction and renovation of schools and clinics, health care, tutoring, business planning, or assisting in other local activities. Opportunities are available in Russia, Vietnam, Spain, Italy, Greece, Mexico, Tonga, Jamaica, Indonesia, and the U.S. Volunteers are of all ages and come from all backgrounds and occupations, including teachers, carpenters, homemakers, physicians and artists. No special skills or languages are required. Expenses range from approximately $350 to $1,995 and include costs of training, visas, ground transportation, hotels, village lodging, and food.

Institute for Central American Development Studies
Dept. 826, P.O. Box 025216
Miami, FL 33102-5216 USA
or
Apartado 3 (2070), Sabanilla
San Jose, COSTA RICA
Tel: (506) 25-05-08   Fax: (506) 34-13-37

The Institute for Central American Development Studies (ICADS) was created to fill the gap in foreign policy between North and Central American citizens and their governments. ICADS is a center for study, research and analysis of Central American social and environmental issues. Three study and internship programs are offered. The first is a semester-long, study-abroad program for graduates, undergraduates and professionals in Costa Rica and Nicaragua. This program offers course work and field internships in agriculture, environmental studies, women's studies, journalism, and other social justice areas. The second program is an intensive Spanish-language program in Costa Rica combined with lectures and field trips emphasizing social justice issues in Central America. The third is a field course in resource management and sustainable development in Costa Rica. This 14-week field course focuses on development issues from ecological, socio-economic perspectives. It includes four weeks of intensive Spanish and urban issues, five weeks in the field, and five weeks of independent study.

Juan Sisay Escuela de Español

Oficina, Y Escuela Guatemala
15 Avenida 8-38 Zona 1, Apartado Postal 392
Quetzaltenango, GUATEMALA

Juan Sisay Escuela operates as a cooperative of teachers, families, and indigenous communities in and near Quetzaltenango. The goals of the school are to provide individualized instruction that matches the level of Spanish language comprehension of each student. In addition to instruction in Spanish, students are encouraged to participate in the social life of the community through projects such as the construction of water purification systems, road building, and reforestation. In the U.S. the school's office is working with Guatemalan refugees to establish a clinic in the orange groves near Phoenix. The school arranges for students to live with a Guatemalan family. The cost is $100 per week except between June and August when the cost is $125 per week.

Los Niños

(See listing under U.S. Voluntary Service Organizations.)

Marazul Tours, Inc.

Tower Plaza Mall
4100 Park Avenue
Weehawken, NJ 07087
Tel: (201) 319-9670 or (800)-223-5334 Fax: (201) 319-9009

Marazul Tours is a well-known coordinator of alternative tours to Central America. Many of the organizations in this guide enlist Marazul's expertise in planning trips to Cuba, El Salvador, Guatemala, and Nicaragua. Marazul is a progressive, full-service travel agency and contributes one percent of the price of your airline ticket to many socially responsible groups through its "Fly With Your Commitment" program.

Middle East Children's Alliance
905 Parker Street
Berkeley, CA 94710
Tel: (510) 548-0542   Fax: (510) 548-0543

The Middle East Children's Alliance raises funds for humanitarian aid (medical supplies, school books, food, and clothing) for children in Iraq and the West Bank in Gaza. MECA sponsors short-term delegations several times a year to Palestine and Israel. These delegates meet with Israeli peace activists and visit Palestinian production cooperatives, refugee camps, health clinics, and kindergartens in the West Bank and Gaza. The cost is travel plus $700. The Middle East Children's Alliance supports a two-state solution for the region.

Mobility International U.S.A.
P.O. Box 10767
Eugene, OR 97440
Tel: (541) 343-1284 (Voice/TDD)   Fax: (541) 343-6812

Mobility International U.S.A.'s (MIUSA) international exchange programs share information about disability issues with people from other cultures. This exchange improves the rights of all disabled persons and increases cross-cultural understanding and friendship. MIUSA has programs with Great Britain, Germany, China, Costa Rica, Italy, Russia, and Mexico. Agendas include meeting with disabled persons and visiting programs that focus on persons with disabilities to exchange information and discuss disability rights-related issues. Many programs also include community service projects, a variety of educational workshops, and recreational and cultural activities. Both disabled and non-disabled persons are encouraged to participate.

In the U.S., MIUSA sponsors International Leadership Programs in Eugene, Oregon, involving disabled and non-disabled participants from around the world including Africa, Asia, Latin America, Europe, and the U.S. MIUSA also sponsors international workcamps that bring together disabled and non-disabled persons from around the world to work on a community service project for two to four weeks.

ORAP - SIT Higher Education Certificate Program in Grassroots Development and NGO Management and Grassroots Development Program

The Experiment in International Living
School for International Training
GIIM Admissions,
P.O. Box 676
Brattleboro, VT 05302-0676 USA
Tel: (800) 451-4465 or (802) 257-7751

The Organization of Rural Associations for Progress (ORAP) in Bulawayo, Zimbabwe and the School for International Training (SIT) in Vermont combine their resources to educate development workers and leaders from both Africa and the U.S. The certificate program, based in Zimbabwe, is open to middle-level staff of African non-governmental organizations (NGOs) and to highly prepared undergraduate students and recent graduates from SIT and other U.S. colleges and universities. The program consists of 6 terms, which alternate between periods of full group instruction (at the ORAP complex in Bulawayo) and periods when students carry out small group and individualized assignments in the villages where ORAP and other participating NGOs are working. The Grassroots Development Semester Program is open to college juniors and seniors, and it follows the same format as the certificate program for the first four months.

Our Developing World
13004 Paseo Presada
Saratoga, CA 95070
Tel: (408) 379-4431   Fax: (408) 376-0755

Our Developing World's (ODW) main focus is working with U.S. teachers to create curricula about Third World countries and cultures. Once a year ODW leads study tours. Past destinations have included: Cuba, Nicaragua, Honduras, Mozambique, Zimbabwe, South Africa, the Philippines, Vietnam, Cambodia, Laos, Guatemala, El Salvador and Hawaii. The tours provide an opportunity to talk with peasants, workers, women's associations, health workers, and co-op members, as well as a chance to learn about health, human rights and educational campaigns, agrarian reform, and economic and social planning.

Plowshares Institute
P.O. Box 243
Simsbury, CT 06070
Tel: (203) 651-4304   Fax: (860) 651-0304

Plowshares tours initiate cross-cultural dialogue between First and Third World peoples. Participants commit to both advance preparation and community education work upon their return. Trip itineraries include meetings with religious and civic leaders, home-stay experiences, and visits to development projects. The Institute plans 2 to 3 week programs to Africa, South and Southeast Asia, India, Australia and the South Pacific.

Servas
11 John Street, #407
New York, NY 10038
Tel: (212) 267-0252

Servas is an international cooperative system of hosts and travelers established to help build world peace by providing opportunities for personal contact among people of diverse cultures and backgrounds. Travelers are invited to share life in the home and community and their concerns about social and international problems. Membership application for travelers consists of: an interview, two character references, and a $55 membership fee per adult. Prospective hosts must also be interviewed and fill out an application. To receive an application, send a stamped, self-addressed envelope.

Third World Opportunities Program
1363 Sommermont Drive
El Cajon, CA 92021
Tel: (619) 449-9381

Third World Opportunities Program (TWO) is a hunger and poverty awareness program designed to provide opportunities for appropriate responses to human need. It seeks to encourage sensitivity to life in the Third World; intentional reflection on our relationship with Third World people; effective work projects that offer practical services to the hungry, homeless and the poor; and organized efforts to change existing conditions. TWO offers a two-pronged program consisting of an awareness tour along the U.S./Mexico border followed by a short-term work project such as a six-day house building project. The house building is with Habitat for Humanity in Tijuana, Mexico, mainly during spring and summer months.

U.S.-Indochina Reconciliation Project
25 West 45th Street, #1201
New York, NY 10036
Tel: (212) 764-3925   Fax: (212) 764-3896
Telex: 6503102691 MCI UW
email: usindo@igc.apc.org

U.S.-Indochina Reconciliation Project (USIRP) promotes reconciliation between the U.S., Viet Nam, Laos, and Cambodia. USIRP leads delegations of academics, students, and professionals of various backgrounds and assists others who wish to organize their own groups.

Venceremos Brigade
P.O. Box 673
New York, NY 10035
Tel: (212) 228-6000, Ext.503

Venceremos Brigade participants travel for 2 weeks in Cuba, visiting schools, factories, clinics, and hospitals; having informal visits and discussions with Cubans; and participating in educational seminars with representatives from other countries. Brigade members participate in workcamp activities. Each participant must be at least 18 years old, have a valid U.S. passport, be a U.S. citizen, and not currently in the military service. Upon acceptance, participants attend a required series of preparatory sessions and commit to work in some aspect of Brigade education projects upon return. They are expected to pay all transportation and miscellaneous expenses. Brigade committees are located in various areas throughout the U.S.

Voices on the Border Educational Delegations
P.O. Box 53081, Temple Heights Station
Washington, D.C. 20009
Tel: (202) 529-2912   Fax: (202) 529-0897

Voices on the Border promotes contact between the repatriated communities in eastern El Salvador and interested individuals in the U.S. Voices on the Border organizes U.S. delegations to these Salvadoran communities. Delegations generally last for 10 days and take place 5 times a year. Total cost of participating is approximately $1,000.

(Also see listing under International Voluntary Service Organizations.)

REFERENCES

Resources

Patricia Adams and Lawrence Solomon, *In the Name of Progress: The Underside of Foreign Aid*, Energy Probe, 1986.

Brent K. Ashabranner, *A Moment in History: The First Ten Years of the Peace Corps*, Doubleday, 1971.

Gerard T. Rice, *The Bold Experiment: JFK's Peace Corps*, University of Notre Dame Press, 1987.

Karen Schwarz, *What You Can Do For Your Country: An Oral History of the Peace Corps*, William Morrow and Company, Inc., 1991.

Patricia L. Kutzner and Nicola Lagoudakis, with Teresa Eyring, *Who's Involved With Hunger: An Organization Guide for Education and Advocacy*, 1992. To order: Patricia Kutzner, P.O. Box 29056, Washington, D.C. 20017.

Steven Donziger, "Peace Corps Follies," *The Progressive* (March 1987).

Other Organizations

AMIDEAST, 1100 17th Street, NW, Suite 300, Washington, D.C. 20036.

Publications on higher education in the Middle East and opportunities for U.S. students.

Coordination in Development (CODEL), CODEL, 79 Madison Avenue, New York, NY 10016.

CODEL, as association of private development agencies, is a consortium of 40 church-related (both Catholic and Protestant) organizations whose primary goal is to provide assistance to self-determined development projects in Third World areas.

Council on International Educational Exchange (CIEE) and **Commission on Voluntary Service and Action (CVSA),** 205 East 42nd Street, New York, NY 10017; (212) 661-1414, Ext. 1108.

Publishes information on independent study, volunteer opportunities, and inexpensive travel abroad.

Cultural Survival Inc, 46 Brattle Street, Cambridge, MA 02138; (617) 441-5400, Fax: (617) 441-5417.
E-mail: survival@husc.harvard.edu

Helping indigenous people survive both physically and culturally. There is also an internship program, in which interns work on ongoing and special projects.

Grassroots International, 48 Grove Street, #103, Somerville, MA 02144; (617) 628-4737, Fax: (617) 628-4737.

Institute of International Education, 809 United Nations Plaza, New York, NY 10017-3580.

InterAction, American Council for Voluntary International Action, 1717 Massachusetts Avenue NW, Suite 801, Washington, D.C., 20036; (202) 667-8227.

Institute for Transportation and Development Policy (ITDP), 1787 Colombia Road NW, Washington, D.C. 20009.

Focuses on the potential of non-motorized transportation and alleviating poverty. Aimed at changing policies of international lending agencies. Provides technical assistance about how to incorporate non-motorized transportation into development projects.

International Development Exchange (IDEX), 827 Valencia Street, Suite 101, San Francisco, CA 94110.

Supports community-based development efforts in the Third World and engages U.S. citizens in educational partnerships with these communities. They also have internships in their San Francisco office.

Ovum Pacis, The Women's International Peace University, 391 So. Union Street, Burlington, VT 05401; (802) 863-6595/5784.

Offers undergraduate and graduate degrees in the field of international studies and international economics. Each student designs an individual course of study with the expectation that upon graduation she will be gainfully employed in her project's implementation.

The Middle East Cultural and Information Center, P.O. Box 3481, San Diego, CA 92163; (619) 293-1067.

Volunteers in Technical Assistance, 1600 Wilson Boulevard, Suite 500, Arlington, VA 22209; (703) 276-1800.

Guides to International Voluntary Service

Are You Ready to Volunteer? Transitions Abroad, P.O. Box 344, Amherst, MA 01004.

CONNECTIONS: A Directory of Lay Volunteer Service Opportunities. 1996. St. Vincent Pallotti Center, P.O. Box 893 Cardinal Station, Washington, D.C. 20064; (202) 529-3330.

DevelopNet News. Volunteers in Technical Assistance, 1815 North Lynn Street, Suite 200, Arlington, VA 22209-2079.

International Directory for Youth Internships. 1992. The Apex Press, 777 United Nations Plaza, Suite 3C, New York, NY 10017; 1-800-316-APEX.

Opportunities in Africa. The African-American Institute, 833 United Nations Plaza, New York, NY 10017; (212) 949-5666.

Overseas Development Network Opportunities Catalog, Opportunities in International Development in New England, and *Career Opportunities in International Development.* 1994. Overseas Development Network, 333 Valencia Street, Suite 330, San Francisco, CA 94103, (415) 431-4204.

The Overseas List: Opportunities for Living and Working in Developing Countries. 1985. Augsburg Publishing House, 426 S. Fifth Street, Box 1209, Minneapolis, MN 55440; (612) 330-3300.

The Peace Corps and More: 120 Ways to Work, Study and Travel in the Third World. 1991. Global Exchange, 2017 Mission Street, Suite 303, San Francisco, CA 94110; (415) 255-7296.

Transitions Abroad, 18 Hulst Road, P.O. Box 1300 Amherst, MA 01004-1300. A bimonthly publication.

Travel Programs in Central America, Interfaith Task Force on Central America, P.O. Box 3843, La Mesa, CA 91944; (619) 698-1150.

Volunteers For Peace International Workcamp Directory,
43 Tiffany Road, Belmont, VT 05730; (802) 259-2759
Fax: (259-2922) The directory is published every April.

VITA News, Volunteers in Technical Assistance, 1815 North Lynn
Street, Suite 200, Arlington, VA 22209-2709.

*Volunteer! The Comprehensive Guide to Voluntary Service in the
U.S. and Abroad,* Council on International Educational Exchange
(CIEE) . CIEE Publications Dept., 205 East 42nd Street, New York,
NY 10017; (212) 661-1414, Ext. 1108.

*Volunteer Work: The Complete Guide to Medium and Long-Term
Voluntary Service.* Sixth edition. Central Bureau for Educational
Visits and Exchanges, Seymour Mews House, London W1H 9PE;
(0171) 486-5101.

*65 Ways To Be Involved In International Development: A Retired
American's Guide to Participation in Local, National and International Activities,* The American Association for International
Aging, 1133 20th Street, NW, Suite 330, Washington, D.C. 20036;
(202) 833-8893.

Work, Study, Travel Abroad: The Whole World Handbook, The
Council on International Educational Exchange (CIEE). St. Mar-
tin's Press. CIEE, 205 East 42nd Street, New York, NY 10017; (212)
661-1414, Ext 1108.

Guides to U.S. Voluntary Service

Internships, Kathryn Walden, ed. Peterson's Guides, 6725 Sunset
Boulevard, Los Angles, CA 90028. (800) 421-3151.

Invest Yourself, Commission on Voluntary Service and Action,
475 Riverside Drive, Room 665, New York, NY 10027.

Volunteer USA, Andrew Carroll, Ballantine Books, New York,
1991.

A World of Options for the 90s: A Guide to International Educational Exchange and Travel for Persons with Disabilities, Mobility International U.S.A., P.O. Box 3551, Eugene, OR 97403; (503) 343-1284.

Guides to Study Overseas

Basic Facts on Study Abroad IIE, CIEE, NAFSA. 1990. Council on International Educational Exchange, 205 East 42nd. Street, New York, NY 10017; (212) 661-1414.

International Studies Funding and Resoureces Book. The Apex Press, Suite 3C, 777 United Nations Plaza, New York, NY 10017; 800-316-APEX .

Smart Vacations: The Travellers Guide to Learning Adventures Abroad. Priscilla Torvey,ed. 1993. Council on International Education Exchange, 205 East 42nd Street, New York, NY 10017; (212) 661-1414 ext. 1108 or 1-800-349-2433.

Financial Resources for International Study. Institute of International Education (IIE), 809 United Nations Plaza, New York, NY 10017.

Transcultural Study Guide. Volunteers in Asia, Box 4543, Stanford, CA 94309.

Publications on Travel and Tourism

Directory of Alternative Travel Resources. Dianne G. Brause. 1988. One World Family Travel Network, c/o Lost Valley Educational Center, 81868 Lost Valley Lane, Dexter, OR 97431.

Educational/ Alternative Travel Directory (published in January). *Are You Ready to Volunteer?, Socially Responsible Travel.* Transitions Abroad, P.O. Box 1300, Amherst, MA 01004.

Travel and Resource Guide to Palestine. Patricia Gardiner. The

Middle East Cultural and Information Center, P.O. Box 3481, San Diego, CA 92163.

Volunteer Vacations: A Directory of Short Term Adventures That Will Benefit You...and Others. Chicago Review Press, 814 North Franklin, Chicago, IL 60610.

Resources for Finding Jobs in Development

A Guide To Careers In World Affairs by the editors of the Foreign Policy Association. 1992. 729 Seventh Avenue, New York, NY 10019; (800) 477-5836.

Bridging the Global Gap: A Handbook to Linking Citizens of the First and Third Worlds. Medea Benjamin and Andrea Freedman. 1989. Global Exchange, 2017 Mission Street, Suite 303, San Francisco, CA 94110; (415) 255-7296.

Careers In International Affairs. Gerhard F. Sheehan, ed., School of Foreign Service, Georgetown University. Available from Career Guide, School of Foreign Service, Georgetown University, Washington, D.C. 20057.

Community Jobs: The Employment Newspaper for the Non-Profit Sector, published by ACCESS: Networking in the Public Interest, 30 Irving Place , New York, NY 10003; (212) 475-1001

The Development Directory: A Guide to the U.S. International Development Community, Editorial PKG, 108 Neck Road, Madison, CT 06443.

Directory of International Internships: A World of Opportunities. Compiled and edited by, Charles A. Gliozzo, Vernicka K. Lupow, Bob Dije and Adela Peña. 1990. International Placement, Michigan State University, Career Development and Placement Service, 113 Student Services Building, East Lansing, MI 48824.

The Directory of Work and Study in Developing Countries. David Leppard. 1991. Vacation Work Publications, 9 Park End Street, Oxford, ENGLAND OX1 1HJ; (0865) 241978.

Evaluating an Overseas Job Opportunity. John Williams. 1990. Pilot Books, 103 Cooper Street, Babylon, NY 11702; (516) 422-2225.

Interaction Member Profiles and *"Monday Developments"* (a bi-weekly publication). Interaction, American Council for Voluntary International Action, 1717 Massachusetts Avenue, NW, Suite 801, Washington, D.C. 20036; (202) 667-8227.

International Employment Hotline. Will Cantrell, ed. P.O. Box 3030, Oakton, VA 22124. Monthly publication.

International Jobs: Where They Are, How To Get Them. Eric Kocher. 1989. Addison-Wesley Publishing Company. Apex Press, Suite 3C, 777 United Nations Plaza, New York, NY 10017. 1-800-316-APEX

International Health Opportunities for Medical Students. American Medical Student Association, 1910 Association Drive, Reston, VA 22091.

Internships. Writer's Digest Books, 1507 Dana Ave, Cincinnati,OH 45207. 1-800-289-0963

Job Opportunities Bulletin (published bi-monthly). Director of Recruitment, New Transcentury, 1724 Kalorama Road, NW, Washington, D.C. 20009. 202-328-4437

Opportunities in International Development in California. 1993. *Opportunities in International Development in New England. Career Opportunities in International Development in Washington, DC.* Overseas Development Network , 333 Valencia Street, Suite 330, San Francisco, CA 94103; (415) 431-4204.

INDEX TO ORGANIZATIONS

FOOD FIRST PUBLICATIONS

BASTA! Land and the Zapatista Rebellion in Chiapas by George Collier with Elizabeth Lowery Quaratiello. The authors examine the root causes of the Zapatista uprising in southern Mexico and outline the local, national, and international forces that created a situation ripe for a violent response. $12.95

Behind the Smile: Voices of Thailand. By Sanitsuda Ekachai. Ekachai, a reporter for the Bangkok Post, travels to three major regions and talks with villagers bearing the brunt of sweeping changes provoked by industrialization. $10.00

Brave New Third World? Strategies for Survival in the Global Economy by Walden Bello. Can Third World countries finish the next decade as vibrant societies? Or will they be even more firmly in the grip of underdevelopment? The outcome, Bello argues, depends on their ability to adopt a program of democratic development which would place them on equal footing in the global economy. $6.00 (Development Report)

Breakfast of Biodiversity: The Truth About Rain Forest Destruction by John Vandermeer and Ivette Perfecto. Analyzes deforestation from both an environmental and social justice perspective. Ecologists Vandermeer and Perfecto identify and untangle the "web of causality" that leads to the ravaging of rain forests, and they construct a compelling, nuanced argument that conservation alone is not enough. $16.95

Chile's Free-Market Miracle: A Second Look by Joseph Collins and John Lear. The economic policies behind the boom experienced by Chile in the 1980s under Pinochet, and continuing today, are widely touted as a model for the Third World. The authors take a closer look at the Chilean experience and uncover the downside of the model: chronic poverty and environmental devastation. $16.95

Circle of Poison: Pesticides and People in a Hungry World by David Weir and Mark Shapiro. In the best investigative style, this popular exposé documents the global scandal of corporate and government exportation of pesticides and reveals the threat to the health of consumers and workers throughout the world. $7.95

Dark Victory: The U.S., Structural Adjustment, and Global Poverty by Walden Bello, with Shea Cunningham and Bill Rau. Offers an understanding of why poverty has deepened in many countries, and analyzes the impact of Reagan-Bush economic policies: a decline of living standards in much of the Third World and the U.S. The challenge for progressives in the 1990s is to articulate a new agenda because the people of the South and North ssuffer from the same process that preserves the interests of a global minority. $12.95

Dragons in Distress: Asia's Miracle Economies in Crisis by Walden Bello and Stephanie Rosenfeld. Economists often refer to South Korea, Taiwan, and Singapore as "miracle economies," and technocrats regard them as models for the rest of the Third World. The authors challenge these established notions and show how, after three decades of rapid growth, these economies are entering a period of crisis. The authors offer policy recommendations for structural change to break the NICs unhealthy dependence on Japan and the U.S., and they critically examine both the positive and negative lessons of the NIC experience for the Third World. $12.95

Education for Action: Undergraduate and Graduate Programs that Focus on Social Change edited by Sean Brooks and Alison Knowles. This expanded edition of our authoritative, easy-to-use guidebook provides detailed information on progressive programs in a wide variety of fields. Each entry includes a narrative description of the program, key faculty contacts and their particular interests, course titles, and degree information. $8.95

Greening of the Revolution: Cuba's experiment with organic agriculture. The first detailed account of Cuba's turn to a system of organic agriculture prepared on an international scientific delegation and fact-finding mission on low-input sustainable agriculture which visited Cuba in late 1992. $11.95

Kerala: Radical Reform as Development in an Indian State by R.W. Franke and B.H. Chasin. Analyzes both the achievements and the limitations of the Kerala experience. In the last eighty years, the Indian state of Kerala has undergone an experiment in the use of radical reform as a development strategy that has brought it some of the Third World's highest levels of health, education, and social justice. 1994 revised edition $10.95

Needless Hunger: Voices from a Bangladesh Village by James Boyce and Betsy Hartmann. The global analysis of Food First is vividly captured here in a single village. The root causes of hunger emerge through the stories of both village landowners and peasants who live at the margin of survival. Now in its sixth printing! $6.95

People and Power in the Pacific: The Struggle for the Post-Cold War Order by Walden Bello. Examines the extent to which events in the Asia-Pacific region reflect the so-called new world order; the future role of the U.S. and the emergence of Japan as a key economic power on the world stage. $12.00

The Philippines: Fire on the Rim by Joseph Collins. Looks at the realities following the People Power revolution in the Philippines. A choir of voices from peasants, plantation managers, clergy, farmers, prostitutes who serve U.S. military bases, mercenaries, revolutionaries and others, speak out. *Hardcover* $9.50, *Paper* $5.00.

A Quiet Violence: View from a Bangladesh Village. By Betsy Hartmann and James Boyce. The root causes of hunger in a single village emerge through the stories of both village landowners and peasants who live at the margin of survivial. $16.95

Taking Population Seriously by Frances Moore Lappé and Rachel Schurman. The authors conclude that high fertility is a response to antidemocratic power structures that leave people with little choice but to have many children. The authors do not see the solution as more repressive population control, but instead argue for education and improved standard of living. $7.95

Trading Freedom: How Free Trade Affects Our Lives, Work, and Environment edited by John Cavanagh, John Gershman, Karen Baker and Gretchen Helmke. Contributors from Mexico, Canada and the U.S. analyze the North American Free Trade Agreement. Drawing on the experiences of communities in Canada, the U.S., and Mexico, this comprehensive collection provides a hard-hitting critique of the current proposals for a continental free trade zone through an intensive examination of its impact on the environment, workers, consumers, and women. $5.00

CURRICULA

Exploding the Hunger Myths: A High School Curriculum by Sonja Williams. With an emphasis on hunger, twenty-five activities provide a variety of positive discovery experiences—role playing, simulation, interviewing, writing, drawing—to help students understand the real underlying causes of hunger and how problems they thought were inevitable can be changed. 200 pages, 8.5x11 with charts, reproducible illustrated hand-outs, resource guide and glossary. $18.00

Food First Curriculum by Laurie Rubin. Six delightfully illustrated units span a range of compelling topics including the path of food from farm to table, why people in other parts of the world do things differently, and how young people can help make changes in their communities. 146 pages, three-hole punched, 8.5x11 with worksheets and teacher's resources. $15.00

Food First Comic by Leonard Rifas. An inquisitive teenager sets out to discover the roots of hunger. Her quest is illustrated with wit and imagination by Rifas, who has based his comic on *World Hunger: Twelve Myths*. $2.00

Write or call our distributor to place book orders. All orders must be prepaid. Please add $4.00 for the first book and $1.00 for each additional book for shipping and handling.

Subterranean Company
Box 160, 265 South 5th Street
Monroe, OR 97456
(800) 274-7826

About the Institute

The Institute for Food and Development Policy, publisher of this book, is a nonprofit research and education for action center. The Institute works to identify the root causes of hunger and poverty in the United States and around the world, and to educate the public as well as policymakers about these problems.

The world has never produced so much food as it does today—more than enough to feed every child, woman, and man. Yet hunger is on the rise, with more than one billion people around the world going without enough to eat.

Institute research has demonstrated that the hunger and poverty in which millions seem condemned to live is not inevitable. Our Food First publications reveal how scarcity and overpopulation, long believed to be the causes of hunger, are instead symptoms—symptoms of an ever-increasing concentration of control over food-producing resources in the hands of a few, depriving so many people of the power to feed themselves.

In 55 countries and 20 languages, Food First materials and investigations are freeing people from the grip of despair, laying the groundwork—in ideas and action—for a more democratically controlled food system that will meet the needs of all.

An Invitation to Join Us

Private contributions and membership dues form the financial base of the Institute for Food and Development Policy. Because the Institute is not tied to any government, corporation, or university, it can speak with a strong independent voice, free of ideological formulas. The success of the Institute's programs depends not only on its dedicated volunteers and staff, but on financial activists as well. All our efforts toward ending hunger are made possible by membership dues or gifts from individuals, small foundations, and religious organizations.

Each new and continuing member strengthens our effort to change a hungry world. We'd like to invite you to join in this effort. As a member of the Institute you will receive a 20 percent discount on all Food First books. You will also receive our quarterly publication, Food First News and Views, and our timely Backgrounders which provide information and suggestions for action on current food and hunger crises in the United States and around the world.

All contributions to the Institute are tax deductible.

To join us in putting food first, just clip and return the attached coupon to:
Institute for Food and Development Policy,
398 60th Street, Oakland, CA 94618
(510) 654-4400

Research internship opportunities are also available.
Call or write us for more information.

Name _____

Address _____

City/State/Zip _____

Daytime Phone ( )_____

❏ I want to join Food First and receive a 20% discount on this and all subsequent orders. Enclosed is my tax-deductible contribution of:

❏ $100   ❏ $50   ❏ $30

Page	Item Description	Qty	Unit Cost	Total
	T-shirts ❏ XL ❏ L ❏ M ❏ S		$12.00	

Payment Method: ❏ Check   ❏ Money Order   ❏ Mastercard   ❏ Visa

For gift mailings, please see coupon below.

Name on Card _____

Card Number _____Exp. Date _____

Signature _____

Member discount -20%	$ _____
CA Residents 8.25%	$ _____
SUBTOTAL	$ _____
Postage/15%-UPS/20% ($2 min.)	$ _____
Membership(s)	$ _____
Contribution	$ _____
TOTAL ENCLOSED	$ _____

Make check payable to Subterranean Company, Box 160, 265 South 5th St., Monroe, OR 97456

Please send a Gift Membership to:

Name _____

Address _____

City/State/Zip _____

From _____

Please send a Gift Book to:

Name _____

Address _____

City/State/Zip _____

From _____

Please send a Resource Catalog to:

Name _____

Address _____

City/State/Zip _____

Name _____

Address _____

City/State/Zip _____

Name _____

Address _____

City/State/Zip _____

Name _____

Address _____

City/State/Zip _____

NOTES

NOTES

NOTES

NOTES

NOTES

NOTES

NOTES

NOTES

NOTES

NOTES

NOTES